A book written especially for managers,
supervisors, executives and professionals who
want to maximize their impact on others.

Motivating Others:
Bringing Out The Best In People

Dr. Wayne Scott
J. Thomas Miller, III
With Michele W. Scott

1stBooks – rev. 7/3/01

Cartoons By
Walt Lardner

Preface

The purpose of this book is to assist supervisors in becoming great motivators of today's worker. Perhaps no job in business and industry is more important than that of the supervisor-motivator. This person is a buffer, mediator, communicator and jack-of-all-trades as well as motivator of others. The successful supervisor must master all of these skills. Too often he or she is the "giver" of positive reinforcement and rarely the "receiver." The supervisor is primarily accountable for organizational success or failure when it comes to motivational-productivity.

This book will give the supervisor 12 action tools, or "12 keys" to better perform the most important role of supervision . . . motivating workers. In the pages that follow, the supervisor will discover how to use innate abilities to achieve supervisory success in anything his or her heart desires, learn how to motivate 90% of the worker 100% of the time, and most specifically, learn how to lead without intimidation and be respected at the same time.

Dr. Wayne Scott
J. Thomas Miller, III
Michele W. Scott

Contents

1

The Role Of The Supervisor – Motivator

All Head And No Heart...Or All Heart And No Head

A few months ago I was conducting a leadership seminar in Atlanta for the American Management Associations with about 35 people attending. Their ages ranged from about thirty to the late fifties. As is always the case, it is enjoyable to speak to AMA audiences. However, there evidently is something about the attendance fee that makes the audience somewhat ready and willing to participate.

This was clearly one of those seminars in which there would be a lot of controversy. In fact, after the first hour of speaking, controversy erupted in the form of open combat on some widely held beliefs of a few of the participants. It began just as I concluded the statements: **Human Relations is one of the most necessary of all motivational tools. Human Relations is founded on four main premises — Acceptance, Affirmation, Affection and Achievement.**

An older gentleman in the back of the room rose to his feet. He looked at me with some hostility in his face and said, "Let me tell you something! I have a seventh grade education, I am fifty years old. Last year I made a million dollars. Starting out as a boy I made sixty cents an hour. Today I own a company that grosses some fifteen million dollars a year...most of which I keep. I've accomplished this through hard work and courage. I employ 200 people. They receive a benefit program and get paid a competitive wage. I expect eight hours of work for eight hours of pay. I don't have to give a damn whether they live or die!"

A young woman on the other side of the room rose to her feet. She was the personnel director of a major corporation in Florida. Turning red in the face and gritting her teeth, she said, "You idiot! (That wasn't what she said, but you get the idea.) You're the person who's setting management back five hundred years and creating an awful lot of trouble in the ranks. The only thing that really matters is how a worker views their job in relationship to meeting the needs of their life."

The first guy rebutted, "Lady, you don't know what you are talking about!"

Then, a very wise gentleman from the middle of the audience...gray-headed, distinguished and director of a correctional institution in the Washington, D.C. area...stood. (I had to stop talking. The program was out of my control at that point.) He looked at the woman and said, "Ms., it appears to me that you have just one outlook. You are as wrong as the man in the back who hasn't even kept up with the times."

Then it blew up! Everywhere! I walked up and down the aisles listening to what they were saying until about twenty minutes later some calm ensued and the program got back on track.

The point is that...**in supervising and motivating others, especially in line supervision, we are divided. A great schism exists. There are those who are all head and no heart. And there are those who are all heart and no head.**

Somewhere there has to be a midpoint...a happy medium which combines the best of the past and the best of today in order to make tomorrow better. If that cannot be done as supervisors, we might as well hang it up and quit trying. Otherwise, everyone will want to be a worker and no one will want to be a supervisor. Everyone will want to follow and no one will have the desire to lead others.

Dr. Wayne Scott , J. Thomas Miller, III and Michele W. Scott

Leadership Is The Most Effective Tool You Have

Management is lonely, hard and demanding in responsibility…and, consequently, within your supervisory responsibility. **Leadership is your biggest supervisory tool and motivation is the most important method through which you can apply your leadership ability.**

Motivation in terms of its theoretical applications and pie-in-the-sky approaches will not be dealt with in this book. Being able to apply motivation the way you staple two pieces of paper together will be talked about. You are going to have tools, keys, to motivate those you supervise in such a manner that they don't know they are being motivated. This is important. **It is supervision at its very best -- motivation without bullying and inflicting fear and pain.**

Motivation doesn't originate as a group process. Motivation starts as a one-on-one situation. If Mrs. Jones is going to motivate Mr. Smith to do something, Mrs. Jones has to know what is inside Mr. Smith. She must understand and respect his thoughts and encourage him before she can meet Mr. Smith's needs to want to do something.

Now fear comes into play! This was the gentleman in the back of the room who was all head and no heart. **His motivational tool was fear. Now fear is the most viable motivator there is.** It is just as valid as breathing, but it is

4

totally negative. Fear as a motivator will get you eight hours of work for eight hours of pay for "X" number of tasks at its best…and no more! It doesn't promote potential in a person. It gives you workers looking for ways to beat and outsmart you everyday. It becomes a battle of wits to see who can outwit whom. **A worker who works under a fear system is a worker who is looking for a way to do you in every time they can.** However, fear is a viable motivator. And, if it is the only motivational tool you posses, it is the only one you know how to utilize.

The young lady who was all heart and no head was talking about a pure "Y theory" of motivation. She walks in and praises (strokes) a person. As Mr. Smith comes in, she says, "Good morning, Mr. Smith. How are you doing, you sweet, good ole' thing, you? Man, today's work is going to make you better looking than you were yesterday." She is so good to him that before long, he just sits around and says, "My supervisor is going to be good to me even if I don't do anything!"

What she has done is give this person the wrong kind of "stroking." His responsibility has been taken away. **When you take away responsibility, you also take away the sense of accountability.** When you take away a person's sense of accountability, you take away productivity.

People want to be led. Now, don't think it's not important to be a disciplinarian. If Mrs. Jones goes down to her crew and says "Jump," everyone should respond by asking, "How high and when?" Then, after they have jumped, she can explain to them why. Sometimes instantaneous discipline is necessary to save a life. You have supervisory authority. You should use it, but use it correctly, humanely and constructively. It should always be instructive and used to find out **why** and not used destructively just because you happen to have a big ego stick.

Supervisors And Ego Sticks

If you as a supervisor have an ego stick hung on to your authority, it would be better for you and your organization to part company today. Ego is not something that a supervisor in today's work world can afford to use in the arena of responsibility to further heighten their ego.

There are people who see things in a totally negative point of view. They say the world is reaching the place where it has no meaning anymore. Nothing has meaning! What was truth yesterday is a lie today. And, whatever truth is today is going to be a lie tomorrow. There isn't any question about that. Over 300,000 new books are printed every single year. Knowledge is increasing at such a rate that we cannot keep up with it.

Within the next twenty years, if you are in a supervisory position, you will spend one out of every four years of your life in a formal, academic training endeavor. Otherwise, you will be cast aside so that you will not be producing anything but "X" number of tasks for "X" number of dollars for "X" number of hours. Continuous training is the only way that you can keep up.

We can ask the question, Where is the hope in a world where there are no longer any values? Where is the hope in a world where nothing is wrong everywhere, and everything is right somewhere? Where there are no absolutes?

Consider this illustration of what is meant by absolutes.

Sunset Carson Was My Hero

There are many quaint little towns in our America today. The little town I grew up in was typical of these. I can remember when I was 10 years old. I would go down on a Saturday afternoon to the movies with my dad. We would watch "Sunset Carson." You may not be old enough to remember Sunset Carson. If you do, hot dog! We can reminisce about the good ole' days!

Sunset Carson was my hero. I loved him! His movies were always on at the Rialto. They must have had a special contract to show Sunset Carson. He was about 6'6" and wore a jet-black outfit, carried two pearl-handled pistols, and the only thing he ever kissed was his snow-white horse. He was my idol and my identification with my dad when I was 10 years old.

In my hometown, the religious framework of the community was that movies were, by and large, considered by most people to be a spawn of the devil.

Now, I had an aunt whom I loved with a passion, and at that tender age, I thought she and God walked hand-in-hand everyday...that she had pure revelation daily. She was almost like a female extension of what I had, at that time,

7

conceived a male God to be. She would ask me every Sunday, "Did you go to the movies yesterday?"

"Yes ma'am, I did."

That was when you could take a quarter and for seven cents ride down to the movies, for seven cents ride back, for nine cents go to the movie, and still have a couple of pennies to get a piece of candy.

I enjoyed going to the movies. I wanted to do it. It was a major part of my life at 10. However, my aunt's values were of the times. I would walk into the movie on Saturday with her voice ringing in my head. I would put down my dime and that little pink ticket would jump out, and I would get a penny back in change. And, as the others ahead of me were going in, I could hear my aunt asking, "What will you do if the Lord comes back while you are in there?"

I didn't know how to deal with that at 10! So what would I do? I'd run out on the sidewalk with my ticket clutched tightly in my hand. I'd say, "Now, Lord, if you are coming back, please wait two hours." Two hours, that was all I had asked. Then I would rush in to watch the movie. When it ended, I would run outside saying to myself, "Whew! I made it. Thank you Lord."

Sunset Carson was my hero!

That was how things were. Drinking just one beer was an "awful sin." Now at any cinema Disney's – The Lion King rated G can be seen in Theatre I and Boogie Nights (barely qualifying for an R rating) can be seen in Theatre II. Everyone's ideas regarding values and morality tend to waver.

Most Work Is Done By A Few People

With new knowledge comes insight. With insight comes new methodologies and with new methodologies there always comes change. Change can be like a magnet for conflict. Conflict can be either constructive or destructive depending on how it is utilized by the supervisor.

You are in business to produce the highest possible quality product or service at the lowest feasible cost. This process can be achieved by utilizing the hope within yourself. It must not be stigmatized or hindered by unrealistic parameters such as "should" or "should not", "never has" or "never will." The hopes and aspirations lie in your ability to realize your fullest potential in the "arena" of your organization. Within this scenario you must act as your "true self." A few people do most of the world's work. These few are the ones who really care. They are the few who work too hard and too long until they reach martyrdom.

Who Do You Think Runs This Country?

Do you think that elected officials run this country? Do you? The people with the power to run the country are the bureaucrats. We will talk about that kind of power later. For now, consider this illustration.

A plant supervisor has a certain kind of power. The people who work for the plant supervisor have an important kind of power. The basic worker has the kind of power that brings about the end result of a quality product at a low cost and a high profit!

Workers have an important kind of power. **Consequently, the hope lies within the worker and your ability to motivate him or her.** The hope lies within the workers ability to become an "actualizing person" as described by Abraham Maslow.

One of the major causes that the martyrs are doing most of the work is that we are smug. There is an unwritten rule in the business world that says, "Don't rock the boat." Why would anyone want to "rock the boat?" It is easier to leave things alone. "We can't do that!" "Can't never did anything."

For the person who tries to excel, and to overcome that "don't rock the boat," "maintain the status quo atmosphere," there are survival dangers. There is a danger wherever you turn. The danger is the person, the co-worker or the supervisor who is totally willing to delegate all their worries to officialdom. The supervisor who is willing to delegate all problems and all worries to someone else assumes that only those in authority are in a position to know and act. The danger to the supervisor who would excel, is the person whose only concern is to stay in one place and build their security in life. Nothing (to this person) is less important than the shape of things to come.

There are three constant dangers facing the supervisor: Ignorance, Apathy and Mediocrity. As a supervisor, leadership is the immediate area of responsibility. Leadership is a gift to be treasured. It is your tool to fight ignorance, apathy and mediocrity. The dividends are pretty high. They give you a framework in which to enact your life. The dividends give you purpose and purpose gives you a meaning. **With a purpose and meaning comes integrity.**

The remainder of this book will present leadership, motivation and human relations concepts in such a manner that supervisors will become better equipped to actualize themselves in the face of any and all odds

Who Are You?

This is a little game that strongly makes a point. It is played in a fade-out mode and gives an identification of who you really are. Unless you know who you are, you'll never lead or motivate anyone else.

Suppose you are asked to write on a piece of paper the answer to the question, "Who are you?" In response to such a question, most people write their name. That gives identity. He or she is an identity, a name.

What could we further write down? Let us put father, husband, worker or professor. You might identify with some kind of religious culture. You are a Christian. Let's also say you are a motorcycle enthusiast.

There is not a thing here that cannot be taken away from you. Nothing! If you have your identity hung up on no more than the areas of life in which you "perform as functions," that identity can be taken away in a flash.

For example, your children forget to send you a card on Father's Day. Or they marry, or go away, and you no longer perform in a fatherly function. To make it worse, suppose a tragedy hits them. They are all in a car accident. They all get killed. You are not a father anymore. You don't have that role anymore. What do you do? How do you fill the gap? Suppose you even get fired from your job because your wife is in love with your boss, and they are going to run off together. They are going to get rid of you. So you are not a husband anymore. Maybe your motorcycle gets creamed or you lose it because you get fired and can no longer pay for it. You can't put gas in it. You can't put new tires on it. It is not a joy anymore, so you're not even a motorcycle enthusiast. With all this happening to you, you've probably lost all faith. You're not a Christian anymore.

Now, who are you?

You are still a breathing, living, viable organism. But, who are you, really? What is your mission? What is your purpose? What is your direction? What gives you

13

meaning? It has to be attached to more than those things or those areas in which you, as a person, perform (function), or you are treading on thin ice. Your areas of performance can be taken away from you in a blink of the eye.

It is extremely vital that you as a supervisor understand every one of your workers. Your values have to be commensurate with the reality of the situation in which you find yourself. The reality of the world in which you live.

If You Manage People As Functions, You're Not Going To Make It

I suggest that you read the book *Future Shock or The Third Wave by Alvin Toffler* to help substantiate the kind of world in which you live and the technological stresses placed on the people you supervise. **If you are the kind of supervisor who sees people as functions in this stressed world...you are not going to make it! If you are a supervisor who does not assess workers' performance, but judges them as functions...then you are not going to make it as a supervisor.**

Consider an example. I walked into a textile company while doing consulting work. It was two o'clock in the morning. I was tired from a long day. The textile supervisor met me at the door and said, "I'm going to get you a cup of coffee." I said, "Fantastic!" She asked if I would wait in her office and observe the workroom through the window while she got the coffee.

There was a man out there that she wanted me to watch. The person I was asked to watch had a sweatband on his head, hair down to his shoulders, and wearing a "tank" T-shirt. His five-day deodorant pad had probably given out four days ago.

The supervisor was gone 30 minutes. I think she must have had to grind the coffee beans...so I watched! And watched! This person was all elbows and moving. He was really getting the job done. He was sweating. He didn't even take a break.

The supervisor finally comes back, and sat down with me. She asked, "Did you watch him?" I said, "Yes." She then quickly stated, "He will never work out, will he?" Well, this boggled my mind. "What do you mean he won't work out? It looks to me like he's doing right well. What do you perceive is the reason he won't work out?"

The supervisor said, "You just don't understand. That man is living with a woman. They are not married. He'll never work out."

What this supervisor failed to comprehend is that there are many people in her organization who are not living the kind of lives that she thinks they ought to be living. But that has nothing whatsoever to do with their ability to perform where they are. The only thing that counts is the worker's ability to perform to make you a quality product at the highest possible profit. What counts is not whether you as a supervisor like them, but whether they perform.

Your job as a supervisory person in today's world is to take the workers that you have and thank God for every bit of strength there is in them. Maximize their strengths and minimize their weaknesses, whatever they are. This cannot happen if you have the values of the person and the functions they perform wrapped up in subjective, superficial things relating to their person.

A Worker Is No More Productive Than His Or Her Supervision Allows

It is not possible for you to change as a supervisor or as a worker unless as you are trained. Consequently, a "Supervisory Axiom" can be expressed. Many supervisors operate in the same mode as the person who said, "He will never work out." Their reason is no more concrete than, "He is living with a woman, and they are not even married." They are not passing judgment on performance. They are passing judgment on the person which is not a supervisory prerogative. Yet, it happens day in and day out in our supervisory world.

The "Supervisory Axiom" is **"a worker is no more productive than his or her supervision allows."** Can you agree with this axiom? Many supervisors will not agree. They'll say that the worker just lacks initiative or drive. Why is it that the worker doesn't have initiative or drive? He or she doesn't have initiative or drive because the supervisor has not allowed it and has not ingrained initiative and drive in the worker. It is the supervisor's job to do just that.

The first responsibility of a supervisor is to train workers to make them better than they were before they came in contact with you. This is the primary job.

What happens with a person who is trained and trained, and they still don't respond? Just get rid of them? Some people are easier to motivate than others. The job of a supervisor is to distinguish between which person is self-motivated and which one isn't. Remember your mindset has to be, there is no such thing as a person who cannot be motivated. For you to think otherwise, you'd have to hang it up as a supervisor. You would just have to quit, for that would mean that you would have to give up on a large segment of your workers. **You would have failed to recognize the fact that any one of us reading this book is only the product of what we have been taught, nothing more.**

If a worker comes into our organization with, to put it bluntly, an I-don't-give-a-damn attitude...and they could care less about anything. It is because, from someplace in their background and in their work history, they were taught by some force, some situation, some environment, some supervisor or a fellow worker not to give a damn. The responsibility and job of a supervisor becomes primarily one to make sure the worker does give a damn...that he or she does care, does become motivated, and does have initiative. If that doesn't happen, then workers aren't allowed to be productive.

There is nothing that you know that you did not learn, except, of course, anatomical, physiological kinds of responses...heartbeat, seeing, that kind of thing. **Your**

Dr. Wayne Scott , J. Thomas Miller, III and Michele W. Scott

whole action, interaction and reaction in a work environment are molded by what you've been taught. You react on that level. It is paramount that you ascertain what a worker has learned.

What do you need to teach a person to add to what he or she has already learned so that they become the productive worker that you want them to become? When you have done that, you are allowing the worker to be more productive because you are tapping his or her potential productivity.

There is also another part to this axiom. A worker is no more productive than his or her supervision allows, and supervision is no more proficient than it is trained to be. If this is true, then what is the most important ingredient in a productive workplace? **The education and training of supervision.**

Summary Messages...
The Role Of The Supervisor-Motivator

1. "Human Relations" is one of the most necessary of all motivational tools.
2. "Human Relations" is founded on four main premises: Acceptance, Affirmation, Affection and Achievement.
3. In supervision today, especially in line supervision, we are split. We are divided. We are schismatic. We are being conquered. On the one hand, there are those who are all head and no heart. On the other hand, there are those who are all heart and no head.
4. Leadership is your most effective supervisory tool and motivation is the most important method through which you can apply your leadership ability.
5. There exist a handful of martyrs who keep everything going.
6. There are three constant dangers facing the supervisor...Ignorance, Apathy and Mediocrity.
7. A person with purpose and meaning has integrity.
8. If you are the kind of supervisor who sees people as functions you are just not going to make it.
9. It is not possible for you to change as a supervisor or as a worker unless you are trained.
10. A worker is no more productive than his or her supervision allows.

Dr. Wayne Scott , J. Thomas Miller, III and Michele W. Scott

11. Your first responsibility as a supervisor is to train your people to make them better than they were before they came in contact with you.

12. A worker is no more productive than his or her supervision allows. Supervision is no more proficient than it is trained to be.

2

Who Is The Supervisor-Motivator?

A Person Functioning Or
A Functioning Person?

If a worker is no more productive than his or her supervision allows...and supervision is no better than it is trained to be...then, **it must be concluded that supervisory training becomes one of the most important of all organizational goals.** The question is then -- Who is this person you're trying to train? In other words, who is a supervisor-motivator? Is a supervisor just a person who performs a functional job? One might conclude that a supervisor is a multitude of things!

An associate of mine says that the supervisor has been relegated to being a baby sitter, a counselor and a

Who Is The Supervisor-Motivator?

psychiatrist. To this list could be added a motivator, a coordinator, a director, a mediator, a controller, a communicator, a referee, an implementer, a trainer, a selector, and many others. He or she as a supervisor is a number of things. However, all these listed descriptors still do not answer the question -- "Who is a supervisor?"

The answer is -- "The supervisor is first a person." **Before he or she is anything else, the supervisor is a person...a functioning, breathing, dreaming, wanting, needing bleeding, human being.** Supervisors are an entity all to themselves. Each is a person. All of the things that were listed, such as motivator, coordinator, and so on, are what the person does. **There is a tremendous difference between who a person is and what a person does.**

All the things listed above are **supervisory functions**. They do not tell you who a supervisor is! They tell you what a supervisor does. This distinction is of extreme importance. It is an important distinction that you must make in your supervisory-mind. **If you see yourself, first and foremost, as a function, chances are you are going to see each of the people who work for you as a function.** If you see yourself in your organization as one who does a set of things, then the chances are you're going to see your people as those who just do a certain number of things...functions, tasks, carrying out certain functional responsibilities.

People have the potential of being motivated, not things.

Dr. Wayne Scott , J. Thomas Miller, III and Michele W. Scott

B A S I C   Q U E S T I O N

WHAT IS A SUPERVISOR?

MOTIVATOR	PSYCHOLOGIST
LEADER	PLANNER
COMMUNICATOR	PROBLEM SOLVER
COUNSELOR	PRODUCER
MEDIATOR	GUIDE
DISCIPLINARIAN	INITIATOR

WHILE ALL THIS IS TRUE -- THERE IS MORE!

A SUPERVISOR

IS   **HOPES**

FIRST   **DREAMS**

A **PERSON** WITH . . .   **WANTS**

NEEDS

GOALS

FEELINGS

The Supervisor-Motivator?

There is much more to a job than that which you functionally do. **Your supervisory job means more to you than just the ability to walk through the organization's doors each day and functioning as a counselor, leader, psychiatrist, motivator, coordinator, transformer, mediator, buffer, planner, communicator, implementer, trainer, selector. And, among a myriad of other things, perhaps a floor sweeper, latrine cleaner or one who carries a crying towel for your people all the time.** There are ten thousand supervisory functions you can perform. However, in performing these functions, **you are just a person functioning...not a functioning person!**

Recall the fade-out game of the previous chapter where the person saw himself as a series of functions...a supervisor, a Christian, a motorcycle enthusiast, and so on. As was shown, each of these functions can easily be taken from you. Consequently, you are left with nothing! Your identity has to be realized in terms of you the person, or you are not going to be "actualizing" in your job. **If you are not actualizing in your job, you are not going to be able to supervise to your fullest potential. If you are wasting your fullest supervisory potential, your organization is not getting from you that for which it pays you.**

Why does the your organization pay you? Some people would say to get a job done or to perform certain functions. Such in itself is only a residual effect of the main purpose for which you are paid. Presumably one might argue that

25

when an organization writes your specific supervisory job description, almost anyone could fill it. Any number of ten thousand people out there in the world could come into your organization and perform the functions of your job.

However, suppose only you can do this particular job in such a way that makes you unique from all the other ten thousand people. **Is it not this particular uniqueness for which your organization pays you?** They are not paying you for your ability to perform functions inherent within the job description or functions that anyone could perform. They are paying you specifically because you possess certain creativity and can provide a unique contribution that no other living human being can.

That's why they pay you versus someone else, not just because you happen to be there. If you weren't making a unique supervisory contribution that they think is viable and meaningful within your own personhood, they would just get rid of you and get someone else!

You cannot put supervisors or workers in a nice little organizational box and say this is your job description. These are your functions to perform. This is what you do. This is why you get paid. An organization pays Mrs. Smith because Mrs. Smith is Mrs. Smith. Anyone can be supervisor "X," but only one Mrs. Smith can exist. They pay her for her uniqueness. She is the most important person in all of her organization for her job contribution as **a person who functions and not as a functioning person.**

Formal Power And Informal Power

The Chief Executive Officer of your organization, as well as your immediate supervisor, has an organizational or structural kind of power. It is a power called **formal power.** You as a worker also possess a special kind of power that keeps your supervisor in his or her job. Your supervisor possesses **formal** power to extricate you from your job. You possess the power to sustain your supervisor in his or her job. Consequently, there is a two-fold or two-dimensional kind of power within an organization. One is **formal power** and the other is **informal power.**

The chain of command in an organization is a power structure associated with **formal power.** Consider for a moment a three-level chain of command or a three-tier organizational structure.

Let us say that this organization manufactures shoes. The organization has a president at the first level and a line supervisor at the second level. The president possesses **formal power.** We can equate **formal power** to **must power.** The line supervisor also possesses a **formal power.** His or her **formal power** is coupled with yet another kind of power called **informal power.**

Formal power in an organization is used in varying degrees from the top to the bottom of the organizational structure and is given with the position of supervision by the job description. **Informal power,** however, is the power you possess that enables you to convert your supervisor's **must power.** Convert his or her edict, the memo, to you saying, "By all that is holy, this must be done

27

Dr. Wayne Scott , J. Thomas Miller, III and Michele W. Scott

'X' number of times in 'Z' number of days to make 'Y' number of dollars. This will be done. It **must** be done."

Now, your supervisor possesses the kind of power to say it will be done. It must be done. You also have another power. You have the power to take **must power** that is issued from the top, an edict, and convert it to **will power** in the worker. So, you possess the **will power** in your organization…the goal, the gas, the push, the motivational power that allows the worker to produce the product that keeps your supervisor and you in business. Your supervisors cannot come down to where you are in the organization and put your product together for you on a daily basis.

Now you have a group of workers who are putting your product together with their hands. Who does this? It's the people on the line. The people who work for you. They assemble your product at a rate to meet your quotas. This occurs only to the extent that you, the supervisor, are able to convert **must power** into **will power**…the power that enacts itself at the end of your worker's fingers. That is the way that it works. You, as a supervisor, can't do it all by yourself, just as others can't do it all by themselves! You are the person most directly in contact with the worker. As the one in the most direct contact with the worker, you're the one who either motivates the worker to do his or her best, or de-motivates the worker to hold up everything. Your supervisory job is seeing that production is done through the worker and by the worker.

Promote From Within?

One of the biggest mistakes made in management at the first-line supervisory level is to promote from within. This unchallenged philosophy has made supervisory jobs extremely difficult and unfair to the promoted worker. **The promoted worker seldom has the essential training to maximize potential by converting must power from the supervisory level of the organization to the will power at the worker level.**

Consider this example of an organization that produces shoes. Bill Jones, one of the employees, came to work when he was 18 years old. He is now 35, and is undoubtedly the best shoemaker on the face of God's earth. He is an artist at his task. He is all fingers and elbows. He can produce ten pairs of shoes while everyone else is thinking about starting. His co-workers are sort of average, but he is a real rate buster. Suppose Bill Jones' supervisor dies or is promoted upward or goes to another job. Because Bill Jones has been here a long time and it is considered good company policy to promote from within, guess who gets promoted? You're right, Bill Jones!

They promoted Bill who has been with them a long, long time. They take this person who can take a piece of leather and smell it and tell if it comes from a cow or a pig. He just feels it. He goes by the texture. They promote Bill Jones, the best worker they have to produce the product that keeps them in business. They make him the supervisor because he has been with them the longest. He has time and grade, or whatever you call it -- tenure! They equate

29

the fact that since he is a fantastic worker and producer with a machine, he certainly will be a fantastic supervisor. They think he will make everyone just as good as he was. They take "unprepared" Bill Jones and promote him to supervisor. What happens? Production hits bottom, and everyone goes around asking what happened? No one understands what actually happened?

What happened is the biggest reason that a supervisor fails – poor human relations. Bill Jones, the former outstanding worker, doesn't know how to relate to his workers. This person, who could produce shoes at a fantastic rate, knows nothing whatsoever about using human relations to convert **must power** into **will power** at the assembly level!

Thorazine Shuffle

There was a supervisor named Susan working the third shift in a textile plant where I was doing consulting work. I went one morning to talk to her. She had been made supervisor after a number of years of working. She typifies this "first-line promotion syndrome" better than anyone I have ever met. Her organization had made her a supervisor, and things just weren't working out. Her area of supervisory responsibility was the spinning room. Before being promoted to the supervisory level, she was a fantastic spinner. Now, she has a problem with her stomach and high blood pressure and is really having a hard time. She wants out of her supervisory job. Her supervisor asked me to find out what was the matter...to see if they could salvage her...because they thought she had a lot of supervisory potential.

It may be that God in his infinite mercy didn't mean for Susan to be a supervisor. Some people can do it, and some people can't. What they had done was to take her right off the line and make her a supervisor. She was becoming a nervous wreck!

I went to see her about three o'clock in the morning. We were sitting there talking, and I said, "Susan, what is the matter?" She told me all about her physical complaints. I asked her if she had been to the doctor. She said the doctor told her that there was nothing wrong other than she was just "nervous." The doctor gave her some "pills."

31

The Thorazine Shuffle!

Have you ever seen a Thorazine shuffle? I have! A person walks along kind of like his or her head is screwed on backwards. This is the way Susan was. She was in bad shape. She said to me, "I just can't hack it!" I said, "Susan, tell me about it, what's the matter?" She said, "I worked out there in that spinning room." She pointed toward the spinning room. "I've been out there some twenty years, and never once did one of those machines say a word back to me. Not once. You see that woman coming here? She is on my case from the time I walk in here until the time I leave."

Susan didn't know how to handle this woman and all the others like her. She was not a people-handler and deep down inside didn't want to be one. She was a "spinner." Now, why, for God's sake, had they made her a supervisor without training her to be what they wanted her to become is beyond me. Would you put someone on a production line without first training them? Why is it that we promote a worker to a first-line supervisor without training them to be a supervisor?

The first-line supervisor is the most important person in all business and industry. It is through his or her efforts that work gets done. It is where **must power** is converted into **will power**. It is the first-line supervisor's effort that creates the willingness in the worker to produce a quality product at a minimum cost that you can sell at a maximum profit. It is the first-line supervisor's job to convert **must power** into **will power**. This is productivity and the reason that the first-line supervisor is the most important person in all business and industry. The first-line supervisor is a special kind of person with a special and unique role to

33

Dr. Wayne Scott , J. Thomas Miller, III and Michele W. Scott

play. Without the first-line supervisor nothing happens! **If you are this person, you are without a doubt the most important supervisory person in the hierarchy of your organization. Without you productivity doesn't occur at a profit making level.**

If profit is important, what is even more important to you? It is more important to see yourself in your supervisory role as one with more needs than supervisor and to realize more than just your need just to eat, breathe and stay alive. You have certain hopes, dreams, aspirations, wants, needs and desires that your job fulfills outside of eating, breathing and staying alive. So do your workers. You have to be able to understand what the person is. You are a person. Your worker is a person. If you come together and relate in terms of just functions, you will find that functions (people acting out their functions) will begin to fight. Persons can communicate, reason together and establish understanding…but, only as persons. If you relate on a functional level, you're going to find negative reactions taking place.

Human Relations

What is the key to you being a person and you letting others be persons on the job around you? **The key is communication.** From this day forward, remember that communication is not just a key, **it is a catalyst.** Communication is the only catalyst through which you get things done. Without communication there would be absolutely nothing accomplished. There would be no understanding   between   one   person   and   another.

Communication is the tool without which we could accomplish nothing. So, we can label it a catalyst. Communication is the bridge that makes possible the closing of the gap between you and your workers. There are also other keys such as leadership, human relations, planning, directing, decision-making and problem solving. These are all management tools. You have to be in a supervisory position **as a person** to recognize which tool you need at any given time. In order to treat your people as persons while you see yourself as a person, you have to have the resources of a given tool operable for you at any specific time.

Understanding is the outcome of one of the so-called management tools, but understanding comes from what? **Attitudes** are the result of the way people are made to behave. **Behavior** falls into the realm of **human relations**. Human relations is paramount to and such an integral part of your job. Human relations is such an important facet of what you do, especially in today's world of work. Today we find ourselves in a transition period where human relations depicts a view of man handed down to us from the 1700's to a new view of man that is emerging and has been emerging since the advent of behavioral scientists. We find ourselves sort of square in the middle. **We are between a view of man as nothing more than a function and a view of man that says he or she is just a little lower than the angels.** Neither one of these views is realistic. So, the task is to come up with a realistic view. It is easy to talk about the supervisor as a person and the worker as a person. But, we have to know, I think, **what the person is.**

Dr. Wayne Scott , J. Thomas Miller, III and Michele W. Scott

"Human Relations?"

In order to complete the statement -- "A person is…" -- we need to talk in terms of human relations. We should talk about human relations with a question mark after it -- "human relations?" Some people might answer – "It's how people interact with each other." What else? Differences among people. What else? Counselor, planner, leader…behavioral scientist would say, work relationship.

What are human relations to you? Possibly the ability to understand and get along with other people? Personalities? How about accepting each person as an individual, and not as a big blob…a human mass? From these various statements, it should be obvious that there is a difficulty in arriving at a consistent answer to the question -- What is "human relations?" If we ask 27 different people to write down the answer to the question – "What is "human relations?" -- we probably would have 27 different definitions. Twenty-seven different definitions constitute a problem…a problem between the supervisor and the worker. If workers are humanly related to in 27 different ways, that makes them wonder what kind of relationship they are going to have from one person to the next! It is possible that they cannot make the transition from one supervisor to another! For example, Supervisor Jones, who looks like a very nice person, but requires stroking instead of giving strokes, to Supervisor Smith, who gives positive strokes to all her workers. The worker often has to make this transition daily as he or she interacts at work with various supervisors. With the "stroker" and "strokee" supervisor. They both tell workers what to do, however, the workers don't know what to expect.

The supervisory task is not to rob the worker of his or her individuality as they are supervised, but for you, the supervisor, to have one idea about human relations that is applicable to all workers. This idea about human relations is a definition of human relations that you can enact in your own particular way as a supervisor.

Action, Interaction and Reaction = ?

Let us examine "human relations" with the thought that there possibly is one central definition and not 27 or more! Consider the idea that "human relations" takes place in action, interaction and reaction. **Human relations is you and the other in action, interaction and reaction.** Which one of these is the most important supervisory element in human relations? Action? Interactions? Reactions? We are probably divided and split. If you have **actions** as a supervisor, you will also have **interactions** and **reactions**. Usually what you are doing as a worker is responding to an **action** above you in the **must power** realm...your supervisor's **must power**. Or, you are responding to an action of a worker. Most of the time in a line-supervisory capacity you will find yourself in the mode of **reaction** more than anything else. Understand that these three phases of **action, interaction** and **reaction** are taking place in a milli-second in your mind all the time. **It is strongly proposed to you, that the most important of these for your success as a supervisor is reaction.** It should be the goal of every supervisory person to be in control of the situation at all times. Consider this somewhat bizarre illustration...

37

Dr. Wayne Scott , J. Thomas Miller, III and Michele W. Scott

Right Smack On The Moustache

Let's say that I am interacting with a new group of workers under my supervision. Also, Mr. Smith is seated directly in front of me and I don't know that I have ever seen him before in my life. Consider the overt act that I walk over to Mr. Smith and hit him just as hard as I can right smack on his moustache. He will topple out of his chair, because it is going to surprise him. Hitting him is an **action**. When my fist hits his face and he becomes aware of it…that is the **interaction**. It is up to him to **react** to that action which has gone on to interaction. He has several choices. He can lie there and say to himself, "Why did he hit me?" He can reason, "He has only known me a few hours of his life. He hardly knows my name. He cannot be that mad at me because he doesn't know me that well." Or, he can jump up and stomp me into the floor…at which time, probably other workers would attempt to restrain us. At that point, both of us might get mad at the people restraining us, and we could have a free-for-all. However, if Mr. Smith cools his reaction, lies there and says, "Hey, how come you hit me?"…Chances are that I'm not going to hit him again. And, we are going to bring the reasoning process to the point of understanding.

Of course this is a ridiculous illustration, but it points out that Mr. Smith's proper reaction might well have controlled the situation. His reaction would have to be commensurate with the reality of the situation. The reality of the situation might be…I'm either crazy as hell or he is reminding me of someone that I don't like from my past so much that I just can't control myself. But, I can, in no way be that angry with Mr. Smith. If he understands that, he controls the situation. If he doesn't understand but responds reactively on a feeling level, chances are that he and I are going to have a knockdown, drag-out fight. This brings us to the important point that the **reaction phase of human relations has an awful lot to do with our problems.**

A Problem Or An Inconvenience

Do you know the difference between a problem and an inconvenience? Have you ever supervised a production line where you had machinery involved? Suppose at one time or another every one of the machines that you utilize to produce your product just stops. They quit working! Would this be a problem? I would say that you have a potential problem depending on your reaction. At the very moment you discover the stoppage, all you have is an inconvenience. Suppose Mrs. Jones is responsible for all the stopped machinery. As you visit with her and her machinery, you say to yourself, "What happened?" Then, you turn to Mrs. Jones and say, "Hey, idiot, how come you let this take place?" You have gone from an inconvenience to a problem because you brought personality into it. Anytime you go from an inconvenience to blaming someone for the inconvenience, you have involved personalities. It is much more difficult to overcome a personality problem than a mechanical problem. As a supervisor, do not make the mistake of turning something that is a mechanical inconvenience into a major personality problem. **Reaction is a major part of human relations**

39

and may be the most important part for a supervisor to understand and control!

Hmmm...You Sure Do Have A Mess To Clean Up!

Consider another illustration about the importance of controlling reaction. A friend of mine lived in Spain for three and a half years. While there, he was the only Psychiatric Social Worker in the 16th Air Force. Some 18 or 20 thousand people in and around Madrid came to the hospital where he worked. The regular psychiatrist got married, and he and his newly wed went to Majorca for about five or six weeks. During this time my friend assumed his patient responsibilities. Consequently, a work overload existed at the office. Also, at home my friend had to cook with bottled gas. Now, you may not understand about bottled gas in Spain. It isn't like bottled gas in America. It is difficult to get the bottle replaced. You could only have one bottle...you couldn't have two. When it started to run low, it was necessary to take it loose from the stove and get it refilled.

It was during this work overload period that a female patient who had come back from Wiesbaden, Germany, on an aerovac. She had been sent there about two weeks before, right after the psychiatrist had gone on vacation.

Her prognosis was as a psychotic depressive with suicidal tendencies. She had tried to kill herself three or four times. When she got to Wiesbaden, they said she wasn't depressive at all and had no suicidal tendencies...that she had a character disorder. They put her on the airplane and sent her back home. She came in about two o'clock in the afternoon. Her husband picked her up and took her to their house on the base and left. He told her he'd be back about 5:30. It was then about 3 p.m. The first thing she did was to go into the kitchen, open up her oven (she didn't even take off her coat), stick her head in it and turn on the gas. Fortunately, the husband just happened to have stopped by the refrigerator on the way out. He saw there wasn't any milk, so he made a quick trip to the commissary, picked up the milk, and went back to the house. There she was...unconscious with her head in the oven. Next came the crisis of getting her to the hospital and getting her admitted. She was crying and all in hysterics. That was the kind of day my friend had had building up to the story I'm going to relate to you.

My friend left for home that afternoon very late, drove 30 miles through Madrid, dodging cows, pigs, hogs, sheep and people, and finally arrived home, walked in and there was dinner on the table...lasagna. He loved it! Around the table sat his two sons, Mike (18 months) and Jeff (five months). As they were sitting there, he said to his wife, "Darling, why don't you go down tomorrow and get some bottled gas? We are running out." She said, "I can't." "You can't? Well, I know you are going somewhere tomorrow." She said, "No." "Well, darling, you know where it is. You just go down Jose Antonio, turn right by the Plaza Hotel. Maybe it will take thirty minutes. I'll leave the car and ride with someone else." She said, "No, I can't go." "Okay, darling, you must have a problem. Why can't you go?" "I just can't, that's why."

Dr. Wayne Scott , J. Thomas Miller, III and Michele W. Scott

IN

ORDER

TO

CONTROL

COOL IT WITH YOUR

-- R E A C T I O N --

BE SURE YOU

U N D E R S T A N D

BEFORE YOU

R E A C T

He considered his day and said, "I'm sorry you have got to get the gas." "I am not going to get it!" Well, the truth is, have you ever just, you know, had to do something or come apart at the seams? I'll tell you what he did. With just one swoop, he grabbed for the lasagna plate. His revolving arm cleared the table of everything that was on it as he came up with the lasagna plate and hurled it with increasing velocity. It hit the corner wall, peeled off striking the other wall and sprinkled glass on the floor. Well, baby Jeff laughed! He thought it was the funniest thing he had ever seen. Little Mike was just flabbergasted with his jaw down to his naval. My friend's wife reached over and picked up Jeff, and put him on her hip, grabbed Mike by the hand, and walked right over to the door. She looked straight at her husband and said, **"Hmmm, you sure do have a mess to clean up!"**

Now, she reacted correctly. All he wanted was for his wife to say one word, and he would have put her on the wall. POW! But she cooled it. Why? Because she understood what was going on. By the way, guess who got the gas? That's right, he did! Her reaction was such that she kept things on the right level. She understood him as a person...and the way he was feeling...and the pressure he was under. So, to the **action** and the **interaction**, she reacted in such a way that she was in control of the further action and **reaction**. **Controlling the reaction is extremely important for you as a supervisor.**

Dr. Wayne Scott , J. Thomas Miller, III and Michele W. Scott

Leave Me Alone, That's Not My Job

There was a supervisor who was shorthanded by two workers one morning. In attendance was a big, tall loom fixer about 27 years old. He was one of the nicest, kindest, innocuous fellows you ever met. He was good on the job, never late, always there, and very dependable. He never said a harsh word to anyone. This particular morning he was pushed up under a loom fixing it. The supervisor came over and said, "I have two weavers out. I want you to go over there and start two looms." The worker on the floor said, "Leave me alone. That is not my job. This is my job. If you make me do that, you might as well fire me, cause I will quit, anyhow." The supervisor saw that there were two or three other people around (audience). He hit in on the guy on the floor like a chicken on a June bug. The guy on the floor didn't do anything but slide out from under the machine, stand up, and, when he stood, he just kept on standing. The supervisor was about five feet eight inches, and the fellow hit that supervisor in the mouth just as hard as he could and took out almost every tooth in his head. He then picked up his tool bag and left.

What the supervisor didn't understand was that the worker's wife had left at two o'clock in the morning with another man. This guy was a little upset. All he wanted was someone to hit! And the supervisor happened to be the person that ran his mouth enough to get hit. Not only is it not elegant, it is also dangerous not to control the **reaction**.

The supervisor should have thought to himself. "Is this normal behavior for this young man here on the floor? He

44

has worked for me for three years." He, then, would have said to himself, "No, this is not normal behavior for him to refuse to do anything." **If you don't understand what is happening in a supervisory situation, then you do not know how to react. So, before you react, understand what is really going on.**

A Person Is A Two-Pronged Being

Human relations is extremely important to you as a supervisor. Human relations may well be the key to everything. How you react to human situations is the difference between whether or not you will succeed or fail as a supervisor. **Recalling that human relations is you and the other in action, interaction and reaction,** then **our goal as a supervisor is to discover what we do, what they do, and why.** Now, the **why** is most important. **If you don't understand why something is happening, then you don't understand what is happening.** And, unless you can understand what's happening, you cannot react to it commensurate with the reality of the situation…thus, you are not going to be in control of the supervisory situation.

As in the previous illustration of the supervisor being hit square on his moustache, his best reaction, in order to keep control, should have been to stop and think for a moment, "What's happening here?" If the supervisor doesn't understand, then he or she needs to find out. The question to the supervisor should have been, "Why did you hit me, man?" Right? It may be that the supervisor doesn't know why. So, together the worker and supervisor can begin to relate through a whole new set of actions, interactions and reactions.

Workers are people not functions. This being the case, we have to find out -- "What is a person?" Number one, a person is a product of his or her learned behavior. Unless you can tell me something that you know that you didn't learn, we will have to assume, at least in a work situation, that people are a product of what they know and nothing more. We act on what we know, and when we run out of knowledge, we run out of the ability to react in the reality of the situation. **It seems very necessary that in today's world, we, as supervisors, have to discover what it means to be a person.**

The idea of "person" is more important now that it has been in a number of years. It isn't that workers no longer give a damn, as recent articles in several national magazines have indicated. It is that **workers do give a damn, but only about what they are doing and its meaning to their lives and to society at large.** Workers are more "we" conscious than ever before. We are more "contributory conscious" than ever before. We want to make sure that our one and only life cycle is making a contribution to the whole social structure. It is very important to decide what it is that makes up the person. You as a supervisor are a special person. The worker is a special person. Together you collectively make up the workforce that produces the product that we sell around the world to make a profit that keeps our business in the black. So…what are these persons? These workers? It is necessary to discover what a person is if we are going to understand what motivate then in a positive and productive way.

A person is a two-pronged being. A person is a two-faceted, two-natured being composed of certain basic ingredients and certain basic needs that every human being, no matter how individual he or she is, must have. **What are these needs? One is emotional and the other is physical.** With regard to motivating this person, we have to understand which of these is most important at the particular time that we are trying to motivate the worker. In enacting our human relations, which of these is the most important? The physical or the emotional? Let's consider each for a moment.

What are the basic physical things that any human being must have in order to survive? What is the first level of physical needs? Air, water and food make up the first level on a hierarchy of needs. Abraham Maslow put these as the basic physiological needs. Now, if air, water and food are taken away from you, you die.

Also, there are certain emotional things you must have in order to maintain your emotional, spiritual, psychic self in good health. If you don't have these certain emotional things, you will wind up just as grotesquely deformed, only in a different kind of way, as you would wind up grotesquely deformed if you didn't have the right vitamins, the right amount of water or the right amount of air. You would become just as much a cripple. On the one hand, a physical cripple…on the other hand, an emotional cripple.

Dr. Wayne Scott, J. Thomas Miller, III and Michele W. Scott

You have a lot of emotional cripples working for you. They're working for you and trying to get well, but they come to work crippled. **Your supervisory task is to provide for their fulfillment in order to maximize strength and minimize weakness...to maximize output and minimize cost.**

Summary Messages...
Who Is The Supervisor - Motivator?

1. Before he or she is anything else, the supervisor is a person...a functioning, breathing, dreaming, wanting, needing, bleeding human being.

2. There is a tremendously big difference between what a person is and what a person does.

3. Your supervisory job means more to you than just the ability to walk through the organization's doors each day and being a counselor, leader, psychiatrist, motivator, coordinator, transformer, mediator, buffer, planner, communicator, implementer, trainer, selector. And, among a myriad of other things, perhaps a floor sweeper, latrine cleaner or one who carries a crying towel for your people all the time.

4. You just cannot put supervisors or workers in a nice little organizational box and say this is your job description. These are your functions to perform. This is what you do. This is why you get paid.

5. The biggest reason that a supervisor fails is "human relations."

6. The first-line supervisor is the most important person in all business and industry.

7. The supervisory task is not to rob the worker of his or her individuality as they are supervised, but for you, the supervisor, to have one idea about human relations that is applicable to all workers.

8. "Human relations" is you and the other in action, interaction, and reaction.

9. The reaction phase of human relations is an area for many supervisory problems of today.

10. Reaction is a major part of the human relations equation and may be the most important part for a supervisor to understand and control!

11. If you don't understand what is happening in a supervisory situation, then you do not know how to react. Before you react, understand what is really happening.

12. Our aim as a supervisor is to discover what we do, what they do and why...Now, the why is most important.

13. If you don't understand why something is happening, then you don't understand what is happening.

3

The 4 A's Of Effective Supervision

The Four A's of Human Relations

What can you think of that everyone needs in an emotional way like they need air, water and food? Love? Possibly, but I am not sure we know what that means anymore. Recognition? Maybe! Let's consider several other possibilities – to be needed, security, understanding, respect. There is a long list of things that could be named. But the ones I am going to name are not thought of very often. There are four, just four, that encompass the totality of the human being. As far as I am concerned, all human beings must have these. They are what can be called the four A's of effective supervision – **Acceptance, Affirmation, Affection and Achievement.**

The first "A" is **Acceptance**. What do we mean by **Acceptance**? **Acceptance** means you accept me, and I accept you carte blanche, in toto. It doesn't mean that you as a supervisor can accept a worker, **if**; or you can accept a worker, **but**; or you would accept this worker, **except**. **There must be no "ifs," "ands" or "buts" about it. The worker is accepted.** As a supervisor you must be able to say to the worker with no qualms whatsoever, "There is absolutely nothing you can do that would cause me not to accept you completely, totally and absolutely." **This doesn't mean you have to agree to or condone the worker's behavior, but you do have to accept him or her as a person if you are going to be a significant motivator of them.** You must convey to the worker that he or she has no control whatsoever about how you, the supervisor, feel toward him or her where acceptance is concerned. **The only thing that can happen to your supervisor-worker relationship is for it to deepen until it comes to a point where you as the supervisor or the worker does something that either of the two won't accept.**

No relationship – husband, wife, child, father, mother, sister, brother, aunt, uncle, worker, supervisor – **No relationship grows any deeper, has any more meaning to it, or is any more profound than the sum total of the things the people involved in the relationship are willing to accept about each other.** Conditional acceptance chokes off human relationship. If I say to you, "I will accept you providing you learn what we are writing about in this book," that means you must become what I say you have to be before I am going to accept you. I do not have that right, do I? But, we do have this condition of acceptance (or non-acceptance) day after day in our society. You will be accepted if you don't drink or smoke or chew or go with girls that do. You will be accepted if you conform to my norms!

Often congregations will say of their preacher that they will accept him if he fits the "normal" mold. He has to wear a black suit, always have a little dandruff, drive a black Ford with no whitewalls, and always be a little threadbare...and pray every time they think he should. He has to visit the congregation and wear a plastic smile. He has to fit everyone's stereotype or he is not accepted.

Such non-acceptance is not honest. It is not honest for the congregation. It is not honest for the preacher. It is not honest for the supervisor who has the **must power**. And, it is not honest for the worker.

If in your role as supervisor you have ten people working for you, it is likely that one worker wants you to be one thing in order to be accepted...and another worker wants you to be something else to be accepted...and another something else...and another something else. Before long, you'll act one way with one worker and another way with another worker until you don't know who you are. **Well, you've got to be yourself as a supervisor. If you're accepted, great! If you're not accepted, that is the worker's problem, not yours.** You can only control what you do and not what another person does. You can only hope to understand the situation, provided that you and the worker can establish the kind of relationship in which the worker allows you to understand. Such cannot happen if you "condone." This doesn't mean that you can't condone the behavior of the person. It just means that you cannot condone the individual ... cannot condone the person part of the worker. **In other words, you beat up on the function, but, never on the person!**

If you are the proper kind of exceptional supervisor, you will seek to take the behavior that you cannot condone and make it better within the framework of the organization's work-a-day world, its rules, its regulations -- and make the person better at the same time. **Your resistance to condoning their personhood makes you more significant to them and creates an internal energy for them to improve!**

Recall the earlier example when the supervisor said, "He will never work out. He is living with a woman, and they aren't even married." The supervisor threw out the baby with the bath water because judgment was passed on the person rather than acceptance. **You don't have to accept *what* the worker does, but it is important that you accept the *worker* or there will be no human relations between you and the worker.** After you have accepted the worker, you'll have to affirm the worker to help him or her become better than he or she is. So, the next "A" is **Affirmation**.

Affirmation is a deeper level of acceptance. You must first conclude that **you will never accept the worker nor will you ever affirm the worker until you have first accepted and affirmed yourself** (This may well be the Achilles Heel relative to motivating others).

Until you can look at yourself and say, "I am somebody, with all my faults, with all my strengths, with all my weaknesses, with all my fears. I am a worthy, viable, okay, fantastic person. I am unique in all the world. There is no other like me. And, as a supervisor, I have a quality that I bring to my organization that no one on earth can match."

Until you can accept and affirm yourself, you can never change anyone else. Until you can accept what really is about yourself, you are not going to be able to change to something else. The truth is that until you can accept yourself with all of your facets – good, bad and indifferent – you are never going to be able to accept your workers with all of their facets – good, bad and indifferent. Now, this is a part of your individual growth process – self-acceptance, self-appreciation, self-affirmation, and self-values.

The third "A" is **Affection**. When you have these three A's going for you...When you have **Affirmed** your worker...When you have said something good...When you have recognized him or her... When you have given him or her the opportunity to achieve and he or she has achieved...When you have stroked the worker positively...then you will have the fourth "A" – **Achievement** – going for you.

You accept the worker, you affirm what you have accepted, and you have sincere caring. That's the **Affection**. When you have sincere caring for a person, you and that person are able to achieve. Everyone needs a sense of **Achievement**. Everyone. Without these four A's in their proper sequence and magnitude, most human beings wind up psychologically crippled. These deprived persons are not people who are driven, who have an inner urge, who are self-motivated, or who are actualizing. They are people who are driven by their fears, by their compulsions, by their needs to have these four A's realized. **The basic emotional needs that all people have are to be accepted, to be affirmed, to be treated with affection, and to achieve.** It doesn't matter whether you are a native chasing your dinner with a club in the middle of Africa or an executive in a plush restaurant in New York City sipping a three-martini lunch. All people need to fulfill these emotional hungers else they are psychological cripples at work (and in the world). **And you are the "most significant other" supervisor to them to the degree that you are involved in their needs-meeting process.**

Everything From Closing The Door To Being Blind

Let's examine a bizarre illustration – that really happened. A supervisor hears a noise in the air conditioning unit at two o'clock in the morning while she walks around her supervisory station. The air conditioning unit is in the middle of a great big workroom around which there is a balcony to facilitate servicing the unit. She looks inside and sees three of her employees, one woman and two men. All three of them are stark naked, and they are being very human. She is faced with a myriad of alternatives. Her "supervisory reaction" is very, very important. We're not saying she must condone what the three people are doing. She doesn't have to accept it. But she does have to accept the three people despite what they are doing. They still have a worth, a value, a meaning and a purpose. They are not unworthy beings just because their acts may be, in the supervisor's mind, unworthy. Obviously, from the workers' learning, from their point of view, what they are doing is okay. Or should I say, it is not so "un-okay" that they have not done it.

What do you think she did considering the possibilities of everything from closing the door to being blind? She said (clearing her throat), "Would you put your clothes on and go back to work!" And that is exactly what they did. She was in a very tenuous circumstance. Number one, there would have been the word of three people against hers, which could get into an awful lot of court problems. She cooled her reaction. She was a white, Anglo-Saxon, Protestant through and through -- And this just flew all over her. She was so angry that she could have just, you know, had a stroke! But, she cooled it. She just said, "Put on your clothes, please, and go back to work." And that's what they did. The next morning the situation took care of itself. The woman quit. One of the men quit. The other one had a word with the Plant Manager and went back to work. The situation blew over. It was just that simple. It could have been a very, very big thing had her "supervisory reaction" been wrong.

Achievement...Is A Person's Highest Goal

Acceptance, affirmation and affection are vital emotional necessities for "we" human beings. Often we get these in a number of ways and in varying degrees. **However, the highest level of human need in ultimate terms is – to achieve.** It may be an agonizing thing to discover ones level of achievement. Achievement is the highest human need whether the human being is educated enough to verbalize this need or not.

Do you know who the smartest people in the world are? We grow a crop of them every year. Our teenage children who have a brand new class ring and a diploma in their hands -- they have just graduated. They know it all! They come out of high school saying, "Fantastic, I'm going to climb Mt. Mitchell. I have the world by the tail and I am going to climb to the top. The world belongs to me. You think I don't know anything? You ask me and I'll tell you. I know everything there is to know!"

By the time they are sophomores in college, WOW! -- They are so smart they could write a textbook. Ah, but by the time they are seniors, if they are lucky, or by the time they are in their first year in graduate school, they discover just how dumb they are. They discover one primary thing – **They have discovered not how much they know, but how much they don't know.**

Then they begin to moderate. That is the frugal discovery. The person who at eighteen was going to climb Mt. Mitchell might be able to make the molehill in the backyard by the time he or she is forty. A person moderates. Unless people can find some level of achievement in their lives, they cannot accept or affirm the life being lived. They face the problem of growing old with no integrity.

It is vitally important that people find a meaning, a purpose, a direction, so they can have some kind of achievement in life. Eric Erickson, in the chapter "Eight States of Man" from his book *Human Progress*, agrees with Abraham

Maslow and others. He states that, "Achievement is man's highest goal." A person lives his or her whole life searching for some element of achievement in the one and only life cycle they have. You do it right the first time in your life or you don't do it right at all. The problem is how do you enact achievement where you are? How do you create (provide for) achievement for those you supervise?

The most colossal supervisory achievement is for you to take a worker who is an underachiever and to make that underachiever an "overachiever" through your personal efforts to enact positive human relations within the framework of acceptance, affirmation and affection. Such is fantastic! You then have one place to look back in your life and say, "I have meaning." There will come a time in your life when your status -- as Mr. Smith, the president of a major corporation, or Mrs. Jones or Onassis or the richest person or the most powerful person on earth -- will not be enough in regard to a sense of achievement.

Ultimate achievement comes when you can say there is at least one person on earth whom you accept and who accepts you -- *carte blanche. When there is some person on earth who affirms you and whom you affirm, carte blanche, no holds barred, no conditions. When there is some person on earth for whom you have a sincere caring affection and one who has that for you. When you can say that, you have achieved. You have achieved that which is the most elusive of all human conditions – a relationship person-to-person.*

Dr. Wayne Scott , J. Thomas Miller, III and Michele W. Scott

Family, Religion Or Politics

The truth of the matter is that in today's world a person has few places to find acceptance, affirmation, affection, and a sense of achievement. What are the three major institutions in the world...the whole world? Fifty years ago where did a person get acceptance, affirmation, affection and achievement? From *Family*! Next, *Religion*! And finally, *Politics*! We used to get a sense of achievement, affection, acceptance and affirmation from family, religion and politics. Let's briefly examine each of these sources.

Religion has 200 plus major denominations in our country. We have Protestants, Jews, Hindus, Moslems -- all kinds of religions and religious sects. They all function in some framework or other and in some place or other regardless of their religious differences. Yet, the religious institution has been pulled into the twentieth-first century kicking and screaming like a petulant child. It doesn't have a whole lot of stability anymore -- and it certainly doesn't do much to make a person feel accepted, affirmed and secure on a human level. Rather, in all too many religions people are told just how horrible they are, and church becomes a place where we have a lot of problems. Anyone ever in a church building program realizes the problems and schisms that arise, especially when it comes to deciding colors and things. Churches have broken up over whether to use Delsey or Charmin in the Ladies Room. We have difficulty sometimes being what we say we are.

We compete for money at worst and for souls at best. There is not a whole lot of stability in the church. Not for the average person. We chalk that one off for receiving the four A's – Acceptance, Affirmation, Affection and Achievement.

Politics. Need we go into politics? When was the last time you felt accepted, affirmed, and secure in politics? Probably the last time people felt that was when FDR sat by his fireplace and had his fireside chats over the radio on the crystal set. That time is gone. So that leaves one institution – the Family. And the shape of the family is changing, too. Think about it. Parents Without Partners is a major institution. Let's break the family down into three segments as shown in Figure 3-1.

Forty percent of marriages today end in divorce. Forty percent just stick it out. For these there is not a whole lot of love there, not a whole lot of meaning, not a whole lot of depth – no acceptance, no affirmation, and no affection. They just stick it out for several reasons – children, religion, and mutual property – for some reason or another they are together. It doesn't mean anything. For those just sticking it out there are problems. There is wife swapping, there is husband swapping, there are affairs, there is alcoholism, and there are narcotics problems with the children. A guy has a string of mistresses or a woman has a string of lovers. When acceptance, affirmation, affection and achievement are absent, everyone has four constant companions – futility, desperation, frustration and despair. No one is ever alone. To the degree that acceptance, affirmation, affection and achievement are absent, futility, desperation, frustration and despair are present.

Only twenty percent of the married have any kind of real happiness. Parents Without Partners has a book called

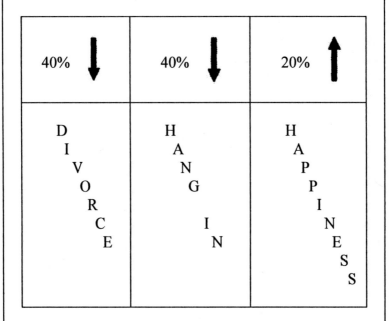

LOOK

FAMILY

40% ↓	40% ↓	20% ↑
D I V O R C E	H A N G I N	H A P P I N E S S

IMPLICATION: Work is the last Social Area of Stability.

Figure 3-1. The Family Today!

Hearts and Morality that points this out. This means that of all the married workers you supervise, only twenty percent are achieving in relation to their family. Only twenty percent are accepted and affirmed with affection -- even in the home.

Consider a scene you have witnessed many times on a television commercial...

"Hi, Daddy"

Here comes a little girl across the yard. The daddy has just driven in the driveway. He slams the car door, has his briefcase in hand, and you know by the way he is dragging that he had a hard day. Here comes this beautiful little girl with blonde hair flowing in the breeze and great big blue eyes. She jumps around his neck and says, "Hi, Daddy!" She gives her daddy a great big "kiss." A voice from somewhere in the blue says, "Yes, it is worth it, after all."

You see, that is a lie for most fathers. The only contact forty percent of the people have with a little girl like this one is through child support. The rest of them have been told by mama that daddy is no good -- or daddy has turned out to *be* no good -- and no expression of affirmation and affection happens.

The family as an affirming unit is falling down all around us. That means that statistically speaking, eighty percent of the people who work are miserable. They are not happy. They are not finding acceptance, affirmation, affection or achievement anywhere in the three major institutions of this country – family, religion or politics. So they have to find it somewhere. They are walking around with futility, frustration, desperation and despair.

When is the last time one of your workers broke down and just started crying for no reason? Has that happened? What do you think is causing that person's suffering? Most of the time it is futility, frustration, desperation and despair. There is only one antidote to that – acceptance, affirmation, affection and achievement. This takes place not in the monetary, physical, functional world but in the emotional realm where we exist. This is far more important than money nine times out of ten. **So, the motivational factor you are seeking as a supervisor needs to be rooted in acceptance, affirmation, affection and achievement.** *In other words, they will be motivated to do for you to the degree your supervisory demeanor incorporates (provides for) acceptance, affirmation, affection, and achievement.*

You Don't Have To Work?

You can stop reading this book at this point and never have to work again as long as you live. So can all those people who work for you. Do you believe that? You don't have to work as long as you live. You can have your physical needs taken care of and not have to hit another lick at a snake. No one has to go to work. No one has to do anything as long as they live. No one.

If you don't believe this and wish to verify my contention - and you are bizarre enough -- you'll get all the air, water and food the world can supply. You can stop reading right now and strip naked and run out the door and down through the plant or office. If you don't get stopped before you get to the street, just lie down in the street nude. Someone will come along, inspect your body, and then cover you up. The person will ask, "What is the matter?" Just keep your mouth shut. Don't say anything.

They will be afraid to move you because they think you may have something broken. "Did you get hit by a car? What is the matter?" You have them thinking now. You see, they are asking questions.

The next thing you know they'll either put you in the car, or being afraid to move you will probably call an ambulance. The ambulance will come and the attendant will check your blood pressure and other vital signs. They will say, "What is the matter?" Don't say anything. Just keep your mouth shut. They will pick you up gently and put you on clean sheets.

See, things are getting better already -- from the pavement to clean sheets. They'll put you inside the ambulance. Close the door. You will wind up in an emergency room at the hospital. Someone will walk in and ask, "What is the matter?" Not a word. Well, that person will wonder and wonder. Before long you will be put upstairs in a room...well, maybe a ward.

No, you won't be put in a ward because the staff members are scared of you. They are afraid you might hurt someone. You aren't saying anything. They'll put you in a private room. If you want air, just make a large gasp and gurgling sound, and they will give you pure oxygen -- all you need.

They will bring you water. They will feed you. Just don't say anything.

Before long, someone will come in and say, "What is your name?" Don't say anything. Just keep your mouth shut. Finally, the hospital staff will find out who you are (fingerprints or whatever), and your spouse or significant other will arrive. "What is the matter, honey?" Keep your mouth shut. They want take you home because they want someone to talk too! If you can keep this up, you will get welfare, food stamps, worker's compensation, and all those things just handed to you.

This will happen if you are willing to play the game. **You (and the people you supervise) don't have to work anymore.** You don't have to do anything anymore. Your family will get fed. You will keep a roof over your head. Your standard of living may drop, but it will be a standard that will give you enough air, water and food to survive. We have inbred that into the present generation? *You have seen that, haven't you? It's called the "free lunch syndrome."*

The Declaration Of Independence

Can we motivate a person using only the physical aspect of the person – air, water and food? Recall that the Declaration of Independence goes something like this: "We hold these truths to be self evident, that all men are created equal, that they are endowed by their Creator with certain inalienable rights, that among these are the right to life, liberty and the pursuit of happiness." Well, the generation of today sees air, water and food as part of that right to happiness. It will be provided. **If we are to motivate people today, we have to know what their greatest need is.** Their greatest need, my greatest need, your greatest need and everyone else's greatest need doesn't fall into the framework of the "physical." It falls into the framework of the "psychological" and the "emotional".

People Identify Working For You

If you are an older person reading this book, you will be able to attest to the fact that you don't see life today as you did at thirty. I know at thirty I didn't see life the way I do now. Does achievement seem more important to you today than it did when you were thirty? It seems that the older we get the more introspective we become. What has my life been? What has my life meant? Why has my life been the way it has been? Then we try to bring integrity to it. *We bring integrity to our workers' lives through meeting their basic needs.* **The basic needs of their lives and our lives are acceptance, affirmation, affection and achievement** in an emotional sense. We already have a surplus of air, water and food. At least ninety percent of the people in your organization are in urgent need of the 4 A's.

If this is the case and workers don't get acceptance, affirmation, affection and achievement from family, religion and politics -- Where are they going to get it? Who will they get it from? Who do they work for? You. They also work for your particular organization. However, if you ask your workers – Who do you work for? -- 99 out of 100 will tell you Don, Jack, Jim or Susan. Your workers work for a person and not an organization. *Where* a person works is one thing. *Who* a person works for is a different thing altogether. The worker identifies working for you. He or she works within a particular organization. However, in working for you, you represent the totality of the system to the worker. If you are good, the system is good. If you are bad, the whole system is bad. You have seen this happen!

During the war, Donaldson Air Force Base was in Greenville. At this certain restaurant at Five Points there was a sign in the window -- "No soldiers or dogs allowed." Because one or two soldiers had caused problems in Greenville, all soldiers were bad.

If the supervisor is no good, nine times out of ten the worker views the whole organization as no good. Well, that worker works for you, but he or she also works at your particular organization or corporation. **Who a person works for is different than *where* a person works.**
If a person works for you, then he or she wants the elimination of futility, frustration, desperation and despair, and wants from you acceptance, affirmation, affection and achievement. The worker wants a sense of achievement, recognition and positive stroking and wants to know he or she is going somewhere. People want to have recognition, achievement and meaning in terms of contribution for the one and only life cycle they have. As we have seen, this can happen more at work than any other place – more than church, politics or family (unfortunately!).

How Can A Person Know When He Or She Has Achieved?

Achievement is such a very personal thing. We often confuse achievement with fame, power, glory and money. These are hollow, but nevertheless, achievements. **Real achievement in a human being is having someone accept him or her completely.**

For example, ask yourself these questions. How many people on this earth do you accept totally, *carte blanche*, no matter what they do? How many people on this earth are there that you would completely bare your soul to? That is, tell everything there is to know about you and know that you are still accepted after you're through talking? If you have one, you are lucky. If you have two, you are blessed. If you have three, it is a miracle. If you don't have any, start building a relationship because you need it. Everyone needs it.

It is important that human relations be genuinely positive in your work area -- not superficially positive through the use of gimmicks. Gimmicks are short-ranged human relations goals. Later in this book we will give you a way to take the four A's -- acceptance, affirmation, affection and achievement -- and put them into a motivational construct in the same manner or simplicity way that you would staple two pieces of paper together.   These we will call the twelve keys to motivation using human relations. These keys will give you revelations from your workers to the point that you can understand before you react.

Interaction Or Reaction?

How do you get a person to interact rather than to react? How do you keep someone from overreacting? That is difficult. It is easier to control an over-reactor than to resurrect someone who is dead altogether -- someone who has no reactions to anything. At least you know where the over-reactor stands. You may not necessarily want to control him or her. What you may want to do is channel his or her energy into something constructive. **The kind of person who overreacts suffers from a lot of futility, frustration, desperation and despair.** When you explain something to the over-reactor, he or she is already reacting before you even finish. In a case like that you need to convey to the person that he or she is overreacting and the overreaction doesn't mean you are not going to continue talking about the issue. Rather, that you intend to deal with him or her on a one-to-one basis.

An over-reactor represents a discipline problem. This over-reactor is probably suffering from an **"I'm not okay"** outlook that is very frustrating. What you are doing is threatening him or her with your interaction. You are making the over-reactor feel that he or she is even more **"Un-okay."** You are confirming the **"Un-okay"** feeling he or she has, and the over-reactor is reacting to it out of anger to cover fear. You really have a problem with an over-reactor -- You can never discuss a problem that can be overheard. The over-reactor will show off or try to cut you down. You have to get him or her alone and explain the problem. The over-reactor needs strong, firm corrective discipline.

A person has to have discipline commensurate to the situation. Drastic circumstances call for drastic action. If you are supervising someone who starts overreacting, you are going to have to control him or her. They are going to have to know you are in control. You must do it humanely and constructively. The first thing you do is ask:

> *What good is it for you to overreact like this? What you're overreacting to is not the problem. The problem is something else. Now, let's not make a problem out of an inconvenience. You control yourself and your reactions and together we will control the situation. But, do understand that I'm not going to listen to over-reactive remarks from you. I don't expect you to take such from me.*

Overreacting is a defense mechanism for a lot of people, especially those people with *"Un-okay"* feelings about themselves.

Efficiency and effectiveness are two different things. Efficiency you can get from a machine. Effectiveness you can only get from people. Effectiveness stems from people being able to have within themselves a sense of viable achievement for the efforts. People want to be needed. People want to be effective and to do the right things, but for this to be they must be in control of their reaction to everyday situations. If a manager allows the situation to control him or her, then the manager is being managed rather that managing. Control yourself and control the situation. Manage -- don't be managed.

71

Harmony, Tolerance And Understanding

The goal of human relations in any organization is to establish harmony, tolerance and understanding. We'll see later that understanding is the key concept to the whole thing. The biggest single excuse, not reason but excuse, that we get from managers and supervisory personnel about enacting perfect human relations is that it is too time consuming. The excuse is that they haven't got time to sit down and try to interact with the people they manage on an understanding level. Well, how many hours of the week do you have to do your job? Forty? As much time as it takes? As many hours as are needed? The truth is this -- no one ever has as much time as he or she thinks. Not ever. But everyone has more time than is used. The secret is how you use your time. How you organize your time, and, especially, how you manage time, tasks and responsibility.

Napoleon, Cannonballs And Time

Napoleon provides us with a good example of how he taught his generals about time, tasks and their image of the time, tasks and responsibility. Napoleon was losing a couple of battles. He got all his generals together and said, "Gentlemen, you have a simple task to perform. All I want you to do is to tell me when this barrel (showing them a huge barrel) is full." So, he snapped his fingers and soldiers came in with a wheelbarrow full of cannonballs. They put all of them in the barrel. Then he asked the question: "Is it full?" And every man replied, "It is full." Napoleon said, "No, it is not full."

With another snap of the fingers, more soldiers came in with another wheelbarrow full of grape shots. They got every single one of the grape shot into the barrel as they filtered down between the cannonballs. Napoleon said, "Is

Dr. Wayne Scott , J. Thomas Miller, III and Michele W. Scott

Napoleon, Cannonballs And Time!

it full?" By now, the generals had caught on and said, "No."

The soldiers brought in another wheelbarrow this time filled with little tiny BB's. Now, these BB's found their way between the grape shot and the cannonballs. Napoleon then asked, "Is it full?" The generals again said, "Now it is full." Napoleon said, "No wonder we are losing the war. It is not full."

In came some more soldiers with a wheelbarrow of fine sand. They worked it all into the barrel until the sand was to the top. Then the generals said, "Now it is full." Napoleon said, "No, it isn't."

A lone soldier came in with a little pitcher of water, and he stood there and poured it in into the barrel until it was full to the brim. And Napoleon said, "Now the barrel is full."

The point is this – If you look at your job and your task and your responsibilities and all you see are cannonballs, you are going to say, "I do not have time. No time at all. None. Look at all these things I have to do. With these cannonballs coming at me all the time, I have no time at all." Well, that is right. What do you need to be? Innovative and creative? Innovation and creativity only come if you have lots of time. This means you have to make sure your time is well allocated and well planned, and that you have the right kind of philosophy about it.

If you think you have forty hours a week to do your job, you are sadly mistaken. You have maybe twenty-five hours a week to do your job -- if you are lucky. Probably the president of your organization has fifteen hours a week to do his or her job, if he or she is fortunate.

Creating And Maintaining

Let's discuss creativity and a new job for the moment. You start off in this new job, and a graph of your creativity versus time looks something *like the chart on page 77.*

In the beginning, you spend a lot of time being creative and innovative. When you first start off on the job you have new ideas, new ways, new methods, new things you want to bring about, new "X" creations you want to do on your own, and better ways to do things. Immediately after your innovation starts, you have to begin maintenance of what you have innovated or created. So you find yourself bottlenecked. Your creativity and innovation level drops off while you spend your time maintaining that which you have initiated in the beginning. And every now and then something will happen and you come up with a new kind of innovative method -- but your time is saturated. It is taken. You have no time to be creative. There are only so many hours in a day. Isn't this the way it happens? Do you see the analogy here between creating and maintaining?

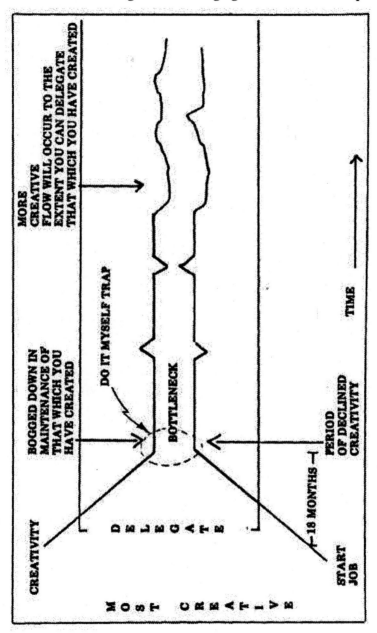

Consider an illustration about a new minister who takes over a church. After several months at the church, he doesn't get around to visiting all the people. His ability to create and innovate is suppressed because his time is sapped. He has no time left for visitations. What happened? After being there six to eight months, every spare moment is taken with deaths, funerals, weddings, sick people, alcoholics, marriage problems, counseling and all those things. It leaves him no time. These are mundane, status quo, everyday routine duties. If he had established any new program like kindergarten or an adult education program, then he'd find that the creative time in the beginning was sapped in just taking care of the job, as well as what he created in the first place. The creativity level decreases as was shown in the previous graph. Instead of spending eight hours a day creating, he may spend thirty minutes a day creating and seven and a half hours maintaining what he previously created.

Isn't that the way it happens? No matter where you go or where you start in the beginning, your creativity decreases with time on the job. Every time you bring in a new plant manager it happens. Before long – ZAP -- all creative changes stop. Creative changes cease because the plant manager has no time to do "creative changing" after having changed so much and having been there so long. Now he or she has to maintain what was created in the beginning. When that happens, progress slows. The only thing that brings about progress is innovative, creative change. Napoleon would say, "Don't just look at the cannonballs, look at the in-between space."

Each of you reading this book has more time than you can use provided you just know where the time goes. But you have to know where it goes. A lot of people don't perform on the job. Not because they don't have enough time, but because they are not being creative and innovative. They are just bored. Just bored stiff. They have fallen into a routine in their jobs and have come to that place where everything must be maintained.   They find they can maintain their jobs in a routine manner. When things get routine, human beings get bored.   Boredom will kill quicker than anything else. We were built to wear out -- not rust out.

Beauty Is Skin Deep And Ugly Is To The Bone

This was illustrated one time to me with a lady who had a large daughter. Now, this book has nothing to say against large people or people who have not been blessed with handsomeness, winsomeness or good looks. But let me tell you about this "little girl." She was so ugly it was pitiful. Beauty is skin deep and ugly is to the bone. She might have been ugly outside, but inside she was a beautiful human being. She had a hard time latching onto a beau, a fellow, a boyfriend. She worked in a bank and drove a Corvette. She went on numerous diets that didn't help much. Her mother got very concerned and asked me to come over and talk with her daughter. Her daughter indicated that nothing was wrong and she was just fine. As she left to go upstairs to her room, I noticed she was barely dragging along -- so tired. It had been a hard day. Her mother told me this happened every day. About six o'clock she went to her room to go to bed. She was 22 years old, and her mother was afraid she was going to be an old maid. The girl was afraid of that, too. The girl's mother took her to the doctor. The doctor did a lot of tests (glandular and the like) and couldn't find anything wrong with her.

Well…in the bank where she worked there was a position open. They hired this guy named Bill, who was not only ugly -- he was hideous. One day he walked by her teller window and (as she told me later) he pinched her right on "her behind." That night she said she came home in that Corvette just flying. She bounded up the stairs just as happy as she could be. However, it wasn't long before she got back into the same old routine of dragging home every day. The mother called me over again to talk with her. After sitting there taking for a while, bless her heart, she told me that she was next to dead. Couldn't do anything. Then the phone rang. It was this guy who had done the pinching. The mother called her to the phone, but she didn't want to talk to anyone. When her mother announced that the caller's name was Bill, the girl came streaking out of her room, and said, "Bill?" She ran down the stairs, picked up the phone, and said slowly, "Hello. In thirty minutes? I don't know. I'll have to check my calendar…I have checked my calendar and I can!" Well, back up the stairs she flew and got dressed to a "T" and went out. From then on there was no more problem. Eight months later they got married -- had the wedding at dawn in her mother's front yard.

Cannonballs And Mundane Chores

There is an old saying that if you want something done find a busy person to do it. The worst thing that can happen to you with respect to time is that you get bored. If you get bored, you have had it. If you allow one of your people to get bored, you have had it. No matter how many workers you have, if you give them something new to do, they probably will say, "Hey, I haven't time to do that. I haven't got time to do what I'm already doing."

Well, the situation is that they do have the time if anyone else can do it. We don't need a special clock. We don't need a special calendar. We don't need more hours in the day. We just need to utilize the hours we have more efficiently.

First, you have to know where time is going. Consider doing the following: For one week keep a time log. From the time you walk into your organization in the morning until the time you walk out at night write down what you do and how long it takes you to do it. If you spend twenty minutes talking to someone about that fishing trip over a cup of coffee, put it down. When you spend an hour talking to a friend about his daughter's problem, put it down. When you make a snap judgment about something because as a supervisor you have to put out brush fires, put it down. You will wonder how in the world you solved that problem in three minutes because now you have the same problem again. You didn't think your supervisor made the right decision and you are just trying to get the consequence off your back. You most probably are looking at the cannonballs and not the in-between space. Everyone

81

wants more time, but no one is willing to do anything about time management; everyone wants to go to heaven, but no one wants to die. Keep a time log on yourself. See how much in-between space you are using and how much in-between space you are not using. See if you can come to the point that you take the creativity and innovation and widen the gap. Widen it out again because that really is your job.

The secret to widening the gap – more time to innovate --is one of the most effective managerial tools you have. What is it? Delegation? You have to find as many of those cannonball mundane chores as you can to delegate to someone else in order to widen the space to create and maintain. It cannot happen any other way. Don't worry because there is no way in the world you can delegate your job away. Do you know why? Because the more delegating you do, the more time you are going to have to create and innovate. And the more you create and innovate, the bigger your job is going to be. You can never delegate it away -- So don't be afraid of that.

Familiarity Does Not Breed Contempt

If we are to exert all of these good human relations techniques -- and we are going to be nice and sweet and fine and understanding and very personable with our people -- will this kind of modus operandi breed contempt? What do you think? Familiarity breeds contempt only if you let it. **Familiarity breeds contempt only if the familiarity threatens you.**

Familiarity is something that is not understood in the hierarchy of an organization. What is understood is your authority. No one can take that away from you. It is yours by virtue of the fact that you are employed in a supervisory capacity. And that authority is yours, no matter how familiar you are with the workers, how much you know about them, how much you talk to them, or how much you help them. There is no way in this world a worker can take away your authority. Workers never lose sight of the fact that the authority is there. If they do, you can handle that. But, you don't have to beat them to death with authority daily as if it were an ego club. **The supervisor who must have his or her authority as an ego builder had better "hang it up."** It just cannot be used for that. Authority is used for delegation, motivation, communication, planning and leadership. But it is not used to build one's ego. **Authority can be used in your arena to "actualize" yourself, but it is not something you use to make yourself a "bigger person."**

Familiarity breeds contempt very, very rarely and only if you allow it. When a relationship is established, your authority is understood. There is no need for either supervisor or worker to feel threatened.

Only People Produce Things

Does "human relations" pay off? Without a doubt! People and only people produce anything. **A worker who is being humanly recognized and humanly motivated, works better than one who is being dehumanized and inhumanly motivated.** We are not, under any

83

circumstances, pure economic animals. We have attempted to prove this by showing you that people do not have to work. They are not economic animals. People work for things other than money. *They work for hopes, dreams, desires, the realization of self-respect, self-advancement, personhood, and the realization of their own lives in their own time in their own universe.* Money is not the only motivator for most people. I suggest that you are not motivated to read this book for money alone.

One of the things that motivates people in a human relations aspect, and one of the best tools you have to enact positive human relations, is to show the relatedness of the job the person performs to the whole of the world. Can you do that for the people you supervise? Can you show the relationship of the job the person performs (no matter how mundane) to the whole world?

The Worth Of Your Job

Consider the job of a floor sweeper or a person who mops the floor. Without the person who mops the floor you would not be able to work in your organization. You wouldn't be able to because everything would be a big mess. That person is important in a number of areas. Housekeeping is one of the most important jobs. It not only keeps things clean and hygienic, but it also cuts down on safety hazards.

There is no such thing as an insignificant job anywhere. If the job is insignificant, it should be eliminated. If you can show people the relatedness of the job to the bigger whole of their world, you are helping them see that they are more than just "a cog in a wheel." They will have a little more respect for what they do to help the totality of mankind.

Air Condition A Whole Shopping Center

I know a person who builds very large air conditioning units. All day long he stands there and puts two bolts on two screws. That is all he does day in and day out. Down the street from where he works, contractors buy one of these air conditioner units and air condition a whole shopping center. While shopping at the center, the worker walks by the air conditioning unit several times a month and never notices it. I conducted a seminar in his plant. And I asked him, "Did you know that you air conditioned the shopping center?" He didn't know that. "Think about it, you did." What does that mean? Before our discussion was over, the 14 supervisors who made up the seminar were able to come up with the fact that they, themselves and the workers they supervised helped maintain the economy of the county in which the shopping center existed. Now, no one is going to the shopping center if it is so hot you can't stand it. No one is going there if it is so cold you can't stand it either. It is one of the biggest areas of commerce in the county right now. The worker putting those two bolts on the two screws had a hand in that. He had a part in contributing to farmers growing cotton and making cloth and selling it at the stores in this shopping center and others.

The people who work for you need to see the relatedness of their jobs to the totality of not only the

economic world, but to the human world as well. This will give them a bigger sense of responsibility, mission, and especially, purpose. This is one of the best areas of human relations you have going for you. To take pictures of something you manufacture and show how it is used in a disaster area, a storm, a hurricane, a typhoon or a tornado. To know that without it lives would be lost is very rewarding. As such you are performing a viable social service. It is contributing to the sociological good of the whole world, economically and every other way. Do your workers know that? Do you know that? Do you tell your workers that? This knowledge will make them bigger than they thought they were. And that is good for human relations of the individual and the whole organization.

Summary Messages...
The 4 A's of Effective Supervision

1. Your supervisory task is to provide for worker fulfillment in order to maximize strength and minimize weakness -- to maximize output and minimize cost.

2. No relationship grows any deeper, has any more meaning to it, or is any more profound than the sum total of the things the people involved in the relationship are willing to accept about each other.

3. You will never accept the worker nor will you ever affirm the worker until you have first accepted and affirmed yourself.

4. The highest level of human need in ultimate terms is that they achieve.

5. The most colossal supervisory achievement is to take a worker who is an underachiever, and through your personal efforts with him or her, through the enactment of human relations in a positive way...in the framework of Acceptance, Affirmation and Affection...You make that underachiever an "overachiever."

6. Ultimate achievement comes when you can say that there is some person on earth who you accept and who accepts you carte blanche.

7. If we are to motivate people today, we have to know what their greatest need is.

8. Familiarity breeds contempt only if the familiarity threatens you.

9. By examining your thought patterns and changing those ideas that are unrealistic, immature or self-

Dr. Wayne Scott , J. Thomas Miller, III and Michele W. Scott

defeating, you can and will overcome much of the unhappiness that you, yourself, have created.

4

Human Relations And Work Groups

Mr. Underachiever, Mr. Average, Mr. Overachiever

It used to be thought that "human relations" was more of an individual thing between you and only one other person. That what happened between individuals was the majority of human relations. There was concern that there was a third dynamic that we were leaving out. The third dynamic focused on the group -- What happened between you and your people. What happened between your people and each other. What feelings your "group" collectively had as

89

Human Relations And Work Groups!

a group identity, a group interaction, a group contact, or a group consciousness.

Within each group there are three kinds of people. One is the underachiever. Mr. Underachiever just never quite makes production, but is a steady plodder and keeps things going. This person does quite well, but never excels or exceeds. He or she just hangs in there – always a little under what everyone should do.

There is the second kind of person that is right in the middle. This person in the middle does just exactly what he or she is supposed to do. They may be a little over or a little under, but he or she is average. Mr. Average Worker. Ms. Average Achiever. If he or she is producing 200 units an hour and someone says to produce 220, this person would swear to you it would kill him or her to do 220. But, if you do increase the goal to 220 units, the average worker will come up with 220 or 225.

Then there is the third kind of person. This is the "Rate Buster." The "Rate Buster" overachieves. No matter how much you put on these workers, they are going to do more than you say. You don't have to worry about motivating them. They are already motivated. They are self-motivated. They could care less about the group. The group doesn't matter that much to them. They live in their own world. They don't care whether or not the work group (their peers) excels.

The trouble is that Mr. Average and Mr. Underachiever don't like Mr. Overachiever. Mr. Overachiever is a "rate buster" and "rate busters" aren't too popular. "Rate busters" are the people who set the standards for everyone else.

Group Solidarity

Consider the following story:

During the closing days of World War II, a very strange thing happened in the European Theater. It appeared that the greatest pockets of resistance were not armies or battalions or regiments – they would surrender in masse. The greatest pockets of resistance seemed to come from little platoons or squads -- people who had been left together away from the larger battalions or regiments. These soldiers had been together for years, fighting to maintain the ground they were told to hold. In spite of tremendous odds, they would not give up.

Five men had been together for three years, fighting in the trenches in mud and snow. Their lives depended on one another. Understand that after the first two weeks of boot camp and soldiers get out into the trenches with bullets coming at them -- they forget about fighting for God, fatherland, motherhood and family. All they think about is saving their own lives – and they are loyal to whoever is inculcated in saving their lives.

The more this group fought together, the more solidarity the group had. When these five people were interviewed after the war, it was apparent that the fierce resistance in this small group was not because they were trying to save the land they held or to carry through the honor they felt or to be loyal. Each member of this small group was reluctant to surrender because he didn't know how it would make each of the other men feel about him if he did surrender. All of them may have wanted to surrender, but they would never admit it to each other. They would do anything, even die, to maintain the group's acceptance and affirmation of themselves. We have come to understand that group dynamics and group loyalty are far more important than individual loyalty or individual dynamics.

Group Dynamics Are More Important Than Individual Dynamics

As a supervisor you should strive first of all to inspire group loyalty among your people. It is extremely important to give them a sense of group identity. While you are building group loyalty in your own workforce, you also have to build team spirit for the whole team.

Recall from the previous chapter the guy who put the bolts in the air conditioning units. He plugged into the whole economic picture of the world. His job pays him well enough so he can see that what he is doing, individually, is important. But he also has to see that what he is doing as a part of the group, collectively, is important. The more people you involve in this collectivity, the better teamwork you are going to have. **Group dynamics are far more important to a supervisor than individual dynamics.**

This can be likened to the question -- Which came first, the chicken or the egg? If Mr. Jones has ten people working for him, it is important for him to understand that each one of the ten people has an individual personality and an individual dynamic. It is also important that Mr. Jones understands that these ten individuals in the group create a group consciousness, a group identity and a group personality. It is like going to a different church. Every single church you go to or any group of persons to which you may belong has its own identity.

For example, when I went to college I joined a fraternity. There are a lot of different types of fraternities. There are Kappa Alpha's, SAE's, Kappa Sigma's, and many others. I happened to become a Lambda Chi. All kinds of group interactions were taking place among these fraternities. Before long you could meet someone on campus, talk with him, sit down and interact with him, and in no time at all know, without being told, know his fraternity. This is because he had taken on a group identity.

You have seen a man and a woman who have lived together fifty years. After these fifty years, they actually look like each other! You also cannot tell much difference between the way they act because they have become a part of each other. They have identified with each other to the point that there is a "oneness."

This is pretty much the same dynamic that happens when people are involved in a work group. If you have a problem worker, the group can handle this person a whole lot better than you, the supervisor can. The group can put the person in line better than you can. They can control him or her a lot better than you can because the group's impression, the group's acceptance, the group's approval of him or her as a person is more important than your individual acceptance or your individual approval.

Every group of people with whom you associate has individuals in it. Individuals have their own personalities, their own individualities. You put these people together and they develop or take on a collective personality, a collective identity, and a collective character. You as a supervisor need to understand each person individually. You also need to understand the group as it pertains to all the individuals. The group has a personality that can be seen and measured.

It is more important that you interrelate correctly with the group than with each individual. **However, the only way that you are going to interrelate correctly with the group is to work with these people one at a time outside the group.** Don't ever make the mistake of trying to fight your group. You cannot. The workers in the group care more about what the group thinks about them than what you think about them.

Groups Are Stronger Than Individuals

Just about everyone has worked in a group and should recognize this illustration. Let us say that you are a supervisor, and one of the five men who work for you just made a horrendous mistake. You tell him he's wrong. He's done something that is dumb, ridiculous, and not right – and it just blew your mind! When it blew your mind, you blew your cool! You walk out and say to him, "Get in here and let me talk to you this minute." The group all

95

says, "Mmmm, he's had it!" You take him into your office and the first thing you do is to chew him out up one side and down the other into little pieces. Then you start all over again and tell him everything there is to tell. You do everything but beat him physically. You walk out; you are just reeling. You have chewed him good. He is in trouble.

Well, this worker you just chewed out goes to Tom, and Tom knows how wrong his co-worker was. The worker says to Tom, "Do you know what that dirty old SOB just did to me?" And Tom says, "Tell me about it." Of course Tom knows anyway, but he wants to hear it from his co-worker. By the next day Tom is saying why you, the supervisor, should not have done the chewing. He knows better, he knows you were right, but he doesn't say that. He doesn't say to his co-worker, "Well, if that is all you got, you are lucky." Tom says that you, the supervisor, should never have done that. And, what else does he do? Tom starts stroking the person you chewed out, and before you know it both are stroking each other. Then Mr. Smith comes along. They tell Mr. Smith, "Guess what that dirty, low-down SOB did?" They make the story worse this time. And Mr. Smith says, "I am sorry." Then the group stroking process cascades as the group sides with the person you chewed out. You, the supervisor, are now the heavy. They are wrong and they all know it.

Why is it that the group strokes the person who is knocked down – "destroked" -- by you the supervisor? They take care of this person. They patch him up. They put the person back to work. Why do they do that? They know that you, the supervisor, were right. You know you were right and all five of them know you were right -- yet, you are the heavy when the group is talking about you. And all the while they are putting back together the person you took apart.

Why does it work that way? The reason it works that way goes something like this. Tom, who "stroked" his errant co-worker first, knows how wrong he was. However, Tom had better stroke his co-worker this time because it may be Tom's turn to be chewed out next time. That is what happens – the group strokes the group. The supervisor becomes the heavy.
It is important to understand that you cannot fight the group. If you do, you will never win. They will "do you in" every time. If you want to reason with a group, do it individually. Do not attack. If you do, you've had it. Groups are stronger than individual people, and group consciousness and group interaction and **group dynamics are stronger than individual consciousness or dynamics.** While individual consciousness and dynamics make up the group, the group influences the individual very strongly. As long as the group is together against you, you are in trouble. Don't fight them. Try to lead them – but don't open fire on your group.

How does one know if the group is sold on him or her? How does one know that the group is his or hers? **When the group controls the individual members of the group to assist you, the supervisor – then you know you have the group sold.** This is a pretty good barometer.

Overt hostility is a good indication that you don't have them sold; but there is not much of that around. Workers don't just come out and fight you. Usually their overt

Dr. Wayne Scott , J. Thomas Miller, III and Michele W. Scott

hostility turns out to be covert hostility or passive hostility. Do you know the difference between passive-aggressiveness and overt-aggressiveness? It is awfully difficult to combat a passive-aggressive group. If you have a passive-aggressive group, the first thing you have to do is to find out what is wrong with them. That is not always easy.

Don't Beat The Group To Death With Your Authority

These two types of aggressiveness will become clearer with the following illustration.

There is this guy Tom who has just been promoted to supervisory capacity. He's been working with Bob, Jim and Joe. These four men have been working together for four or five years. Every afternoon at about ten minutes before five, they hit the washroom and start washing up – ten minutes early. One day after Tom has taken over his supervisory duties, he goes into the washroom, and there he discovers his former friends – not working, but washing up early. This is not really what they are supposed to be doing. They are supposed to be out there working until time to quit at five o'clock.

Tom says, "Now fellows, come on. We are not going to be able to do this anymore. The thing to do is to go on back to work."

His former friends say, "Aw, come on, Tom, we've been doing this for years. You know, you did it before you became supervisor."

Tom blows his cool. He is threatened. He is hurt. He says, "Now look, I told you to get out of here and go back to work. If you can't do that, there's going to be trouble!"

They look at each other, they put down their towels, and they go back to work. There are eight other people in that group. What happens? Production begins to slip way down. Accidents begin to happen – and this has never happened before. Funny little things begin to happen that are just peculiar abnormal breakdowns. These kinds of things begin to happen daily.

The group is harassing Tom. Why? He approached them in the wrong way. *He is now beating them to death with his authority.* The problem is that he used to do what he berated them for doing – and he doesn't show much understanding in trying to change their behavior. When production begins to drop off and unusual occurrences begin to happen with almost no explanation, you can feel in your bones that something is wrong with the group. It is now necessary for Tom to see if he can find out what is wrong.

How should you as the supervisor go about finding out what is wrong with the group? Keep your eye on the ringleader. The ringleader is a pretty good barometer. *Can* he or she tell you what is wrong? Or *will* he tell you what is wrong? No! Then how are you going to find out?

You are going to have to feel them all out --- and it is best to handle this on a one-on-one basis. After determining what the problem is through discussions with individuals, then be open enough to talk to your whole group. Don't ever underestimate group pressure or group dynamics. **The main thing to remember about group pressure is that you cannot fight it no matter how wrong the worker may be. The rest of the group is going to stroke and protect the worker.** The next time it may be one of them.

Use Group Dynamics To Make Your Job Easier

You can use group dynamics -- group participation and group experience -- in such a way that it can make your job easier. Suppose you have ten people in your work group, and you have plans, goals and objectives for an increase in your production – or any number of things to accomplish. You are going from "X" units to "Y" units. You say to your group, "Here is where we are and this is where we ought to be. How do you think we should get there?" Nine time out of ten, if you have the group sold, the group will ask more of themselves than you will. You must let them in on the decision-making process in order to keep the group as an individual entity working along with you.

It is one thing for a supervisor to go to his group and say, "Okay, this is where we are and this is where we have to be, and this is how we are going to do it." It is another thing altogether when you say, "Okay, you have done a fantastic job. I am proud of you. We have accomplished a lot together. Now we have a few changes to make. This is where we are, and this is where we are going. What do you think is the best way to accomplish this?" Let them have input into the situation. That is one of the best ways to save the group's collective consciousness and to mold the group.

If you have five years of experience in a job and ten people working for you each of whom has ten years or more experience in his or her job – that is over 100 years of experience collectively, versus your five years of experience! You need to utilize that collective experience in some way. You need to listen to members of the group when they speak because they probably know a whole lot more about things than you do all by yourself.

So keep your people informed. Let them know. Let them in on the decision-making process. Most of the time they will ask more of themselves than you ask of them. If you are open with a group, really open, chances are they will be open with you. **You can be a group leader only if the group follows you.** *Therefore, you have to make sure that you and the group has a good relationship.*

There are various styles of leadership – democratic, autocratic and free-reign. By far the best kind of leadership to exert when you are dealing with a group is democratic. This is true especially at your supervisory level where you have goals, plans, procedures, and processes that the group is responsible to enact. Be democratic enough to let group members have their say, while you maintain the authority and the responsibility for making the decision – after all have had their say.

101

The Japanese do this and it works well for them. Before they make any decisions, what they are going to decide on is talked about from the bottom rung to the top office, all up and down the whole organizational structure. They make decisions through a process of selling their workers after everyone has provided input. **This type of decision-making takes longer, but productivity is greater and occurs faster after the decision is made.** The Japanese have discovered what we have known for a long time (but may not use!) – People in groups work better for things they decided than they do for things that have been decided for them.

Major automobile producers have done the same thing and the results have been fantastic. Each work group competes with every other group. The quality of the craftsmanship then becomes a "prod factor" in the total group. In other words, if one person is putting on a door and another is putting in the window, these two people have to work together. One is not going to let the other put the window in poorly if the person has any pride at all. And the other one is not going to let the other make an improper door by not putting in the window correctly. This results in a system of checks and balances that works well together. The more the worker is involved in the total process – quality always seems to go up.

The group somehow handles its own personality conflicts. If the group cannot handle them, what you become as a supervisor is a mediator, an arbitrator, and one who helps group members understand each other. If that doesn't work – if a person doesn't fit into the group – then you must put that person where he or she can function and put someone else in that spot. Manpower replacement power is important. What if three out of four don't work together as a group? Get a new group!

This brings up the question of "bad guys." You know "good guys" and "bad guys." The good guys wear the white hats and the bad guys don't wear hats at all. "Bad guys" really can be controlled a lot by group pressure and censure. If there is a worker in the group who constantly is late, ten minutes all the time, the group could help a lot to curb that person being late by not liking it. A worker who is late will do one or two things: either stop being late, or explain to the group the reason for being late, or exorcise himself or herself from the group.

It is difficult to form a team spirit in a group when you have a wide diversity of personalities, backgrounds, cultures, values, attitudes, and morals – all working within one group. Birds of a feather do, indeed, like to flock together. It is okay when you have a group of "rate busters" together. If you put one "rate buster" into a group of underachievers and if he or she is a very skillful rate buster, the chances are that person is going to help the whole group – especially if that person possess a sort of charisma and can become the informal group leader.

Dr. Wayne Scott , J. Thomas Miller, III and Michele W. Scott

Summary Messages...
Human Relations And Work Groups

1. Group dynamics are far more important to a supervisor than individual dynamics.
2. You can be a group leader only if the group follows you.
3. The only way you are going to properly relate to a group is to work with the group members one at a time outside of the group.
4. Group consciousness and group dynamics are stronger than individual consciousness or individual dynamics.
5. When the group controls the individual members to assist you the supervisor, then you know you have the group sold.
6. Don't beat the group to death with your authority.

5

Motivation And How It Applies To You and Your Job

Achievement Is Up To You

In this chapter we will discuss motivation and how it applies to you and your job. This new way, this methodology, this tool for achievement will unfold as Figure 5-1 is explained.

In the previous chapters we discussed motivation in terms of you as the supervisor being a motivator. **We put forth the one single idea that motivates you more than any other is your working "now" for something in the "future."**

Motivation For Today!

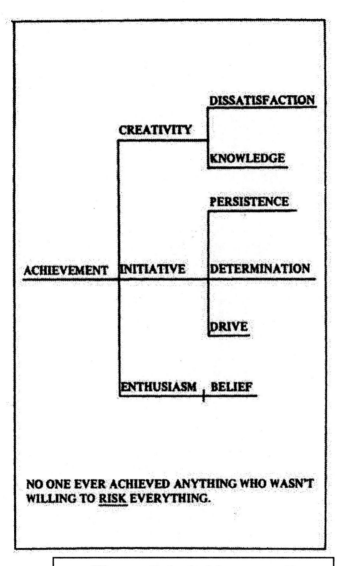

Figure 5-1. Achievement!

What is it that you are working for now that you seek to attain in the future?   Which one of the four A's? **Achievement!** Achievement is wrapped up in three words – **Creativity, Initiative** and **Enthusiasm.** Coupled with **Creativity** are two words – **Dissatisfaction** and **Knowledge.** Coupled with **Initiative** there are three words – **Persistence, Determination** and **Drive.** Coupled with **Enthusiasm** there is one word – **Belief.**

When you are dissatisfied, you are interested enough in your **dissatisfaction** to study alternatives and new directions for removing your dissatisfaction – to make it better. You then use your **creativity**. You act on your creativity through your **initiative**. This happens only if you have a certain amount of **persistence, determination** and **drive**. *No matter how much creativity or initiative you have, if you cannot sell people on your idea, if you cannot be as enthusiastic about your idea as is humanly possible, people will not follow you.* **Enthusiasm** is the mechanism for getting across creative ideas in the first place. Your enthusiasm comes only from being able to **believe** in what you have created.

It is reasonable to assume that as you read these words you are striving now with a sense of achievement to bring you something fifteen years from now. For some of you this achievement may be to sit around financially secure; for others it may be to have a position high on the ladder of management; and for others it may be to do something with your life greater than you have done thus far – something to make your life more meaningful, more productive, more actualized. *So you are motivated at the moment by a sense of hoping for achievement in the future.*

Whatever the achievement is to you, it will never come unless you bring it about. No one is going to do it for you. The five major areas in which you can actualize yourself are: social, family, job, religious and cultural. But you must do it for yourself.

There Is No Motivation Blanket To Throw Over Your Organization

Consider the simple formula:

Performance = Ability X Motivation.

What you want to motivate in your worker is his or her performance to produce. We have known this for a long time. **However, the biggest single mistake with regard to motivation that we have ever made as managers is to hold the mistaken idea that you can take a motivation blanket and throw it out over your entire organization and let it settle down and motivate everyone the same way.**

This is not the way it works. The thing that works to motivate each individual is different because each person has different interests and different ideas toward achievement. **The supervisor who wants performance from a group of workers has to motivate them on an individual "needs-meeting" level.** You have to meet their needs as seen through their eyes. You must open up an avenue so that a specific "need" or several "needs" can be realized. Until you can do that you are not going to motivate anyone.

109

The truth is we don't motivate anyone. All we can do as supervisors is to stimulate needs through a one-on-one situation so that the person becomes motivated from within to perform for us so that his or her needs can be realized.

You have to know at least four things to motivate anyone from within self-actualized motivation. This is illustrated in Figure 5-2.

The four things you must know are:

1. **Yourself**
2. **The other person** you are trying to get to perform (to motivate)
3. **The situation** of both the organization and the worker
4. **The tools available** to you to meet the needs of both the organization and the worker

You will have a mutual "needs-meeting situation" in which performance takes place – *if you know these four things and use the tools available to meet both the needs of the company and the needs of the worker.*

You must use the tools available in such a way that:

- What the worker needs the company can give
- What the company needs the worker can give

1. SELF

2. OTHER

3. SITUATION

   A. COMPANY

   B. WORKER

4. TOOLS AVAILABLE TO MEET THE NEEDS OF 3(A) AND 3(B).

Figure 5-2. What One Must Know to Motivate

You will then have a mutual "needs-meeting situation" in which performance takes place. The company performs for the worker and the worker performs for the company. You have a happy bond between the two. If the company cannot perform for the worker -- cannot give the worker the right kind of stage upon which he or she can act -- then you have nothing going for you. On the other hand, if the company gives the worker the stage upon which to act and the worker's talents and abilities are such that the company does not need them, you have nothing going for you. *The company and the worker have to dovetail in order to have maximum performance from the potential available in both.*

Motivational Mystery

How do you dovetail the two separate needs? There is an enigma in business and industry -- A motivational mystery that we really haven't been able to figure out. A number of studies have been done and a lot of data has been collected, but no one has been able to really explain it to the point that we have a prescription or cure.

The enigma (the motivational mystery) is this. Recall in any organization, there are three levels of workers. There is Mr. Average. Whatever happens, Mr. Average is going to stick with it. There is Mr. Sub-Average, and then there is Mr. Above-Average. Mr. Sub-Average is an underachiever. Mr. Above-Average is the person who exceeds the demands all the time – no matter what. We call this person a "rate buster." Mr. Average meets the rates. He or she is a "rate meeter." Mr. Sub-Average is always a "rate retarder."

This is the problem – the enigma – the motivational mystery that we do not understand. If your rate standard or operating rate is 150 units in an eight-hour day, Mr. Sub-Average is going to do 120-130 units no matter what. Mr. Average produces 150 units working just as hard as he can. When observed by the time-study person, Mr. Above-Average does what he always does, plus he wants to excel, so he produces up to 180 units.

Lets say a time study of production is done and the organization changes the rate standard from 150 to 170. And then what happens? The enigma shows up. The guy who was producing 130 units when the rate was 150, who couldn't do one bit more than he ever did is now doing 150 units! He could never do 150 units before! The production of Mr. Average, who could never do more than 145 or 155 units when the rate standard was 150, now jumps up to 165 or 175 units. The same miraculous thing happens. Mr. Above-Average, who topped out at 180, is now producing 190 units.

Have you ever seen this happen? What is the explanation? Maybe it is a personal challenge. The workers will meet the demands and they will even exceed the demands. The problem is not Mr. Above-Average, is it? The "rate buster" is not the problem. Mr. Sub-Average, the "rate-retarder," is a little bit of a problem. What we would really like to do is to move the "rate retarder" to the level of the "rate meeter" and the "rate meeter" to the level of the "rate buster." We need to consider the difference between the

Dr. Wayne Scott , J. Thomas Miller, III and Michele W. Scott

personalities of each person, as well as the differences in the group dynamics and the individual dynamics.

The "rate buster" is the type of person who works pretty much by him or herself. Not a joiner, the "rate buster" is not really concerned about the social implications of his or her job, the area in which he or she works nor the acceptance of the people with whom he or she works. The "rate meeter" usually grew up in an urban environment where group participation was important – where being a part of a larger organization was very important to him or her. Conformity is important. The "rate buster" and the "rate retarder" have quite an influence on each other, but neither of these have much influence on the "rate meeter." It seems that the "rate buster" and the "rate retarder" have little associations with the "rate meeter." They could care less what is thought of them. What the "rate buster" thinks of him or herself seems to be more important than what the other two think. However, what the group thinks is very important. They will bind together in a kind of mutual group dynamics that gives solidarity within the organization.

Each of these groups is made up of individual people. "Rate busters" are individuals, "rate meeters" are individuals, and "rate retarders" are individuals. Each illustrates the motivational mystery of how a person can produce at one level and then as the company shifts the standard of production, each group shifts its average accordingly – to a level that was previously impossible. We know based on these mystery dynamics that everyone can do more than he or she is doing.

114

Incentive programs do not always work well. The offer of more money as an incentive is okay for some groups. The "rate buster" group will flat eat it up. But the "rate meeters" and the "rate retarders" establish what the needs of their lives are for a particular time, and they begin to live within the context of those needs in comfort, maintaining the status quo. However all people can improve if they are given some kind of motivational support. Just as you, the supervisor, have a goal to reach for fifteen years from now, the workers need someone to help them identify a future goal and the fact that this goal (their own goal) is a realizable goal.

Making "Rate Busters" Out Of Everyone

How can we move the "rate retarder" and the "rate meeter" groups into the "rate buster" group? Remember, motivation takes place on a "needs meeting" level and nowhere else. We said previously that about **the only thing a supervisor can do very realistically is offer the worker a stage upon which he or she can enable him or herself to self-actualization** – whether or not the worker is a "rate retarder," a "rate meeter" or a "rate buster." What do we mean? The first thing that we have to look at is the person's need – for acceptance, affirmation, affection, and achievement.

Each individual is driven his or her entire life by certain basic psychological needs and drives. To understand people in general you should be aware of these forces that impel the person to act and perform in a certain manner.

115

Dr. Wayne Scott , J. Thomas Miller, III and Michele W. Scott

With knowledge of Abraham Maslow's Hierarchy of Needs, as shown in Figure 5-3 you can gain insight and empathy and become aware of the individual's cognitive processes. Maslow's Hierarchy of Needs are condensed from the usual seven to five levels for this discussion.

1. **Basic Physical Needs:** Basic physical needs include air, water, food and shelter.

2. **Safety and Security:** The need for life and the preservation of life are the basics of this level. Economic security enters in not so much for money but for what money can buy. Safety precautions, medical check-ups, and concern for a long life are direct expressions of this basic need.

3. **Social:** The need to belong, to love and be loved, to be a member of a group, to be accepted are all included in the social level. As a higher level need than that of security, social concerns become increasingly important, as the major security needs are basically satisfied.

4. **Esteem:** This level includes the need to have esteem of two kinds – esteem from others and of self. Esteem from others is at a higher level than belonging (social level) because it involves not only being a member of a group, but also being a *valued* member of the group. It is not the desire to do a good job, but rather to be recognized for doing a good job. Self-esteem is the need to value one's self – it is enhanced by being "in the know" and to have some measure of control over what happens to one's self.

5. **Self-Actualization:** At this level the focus is on the need to become the best that one can become, to develop one's own potentialities, to grow into a higher-order human being, to internalize a value system, and to experience growth. Maslow says that people concerned with these needs are "meta-motivated" and are devoted to some task, call, vocation, beloved work – outside themselves.

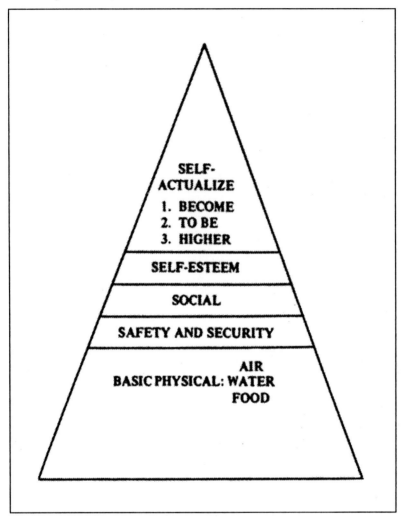

Figure 5-3. Maslow's
Motivational Needs

Motivation... In The Absence Of Promotion

There is a woman in a particular job level. Her job level has been static for some time and you cannot dangle in front of her the opportunity of a higher-level job no matter how good she may be in her job. For circumstances beyond your control, there are no openings. She cannot jump the chain of command and she doesn't have seniority. For whatever reason, you cannot say to her, you do "X" number of tasks in superlative quality and you are assured of a promotion. The question is – How do you keep this person motivated?

You need to give this woman as much peripheral responsibility, within the framework of her job, as you possibly can. You keep her motivated at two levels:

1. You can provide a sort of security on the one hand. Even though you cannot offer her a carrot, you can offer her security and stability, which are part of ones need level.
2. You can offer her the ability to expand her knowledge, maybe cross-train her in something on her own time.

You can add to her responsibility – make her an unofficial assistant to you. You can enlarge her job and give more responsibility without giving more pay. Some people will go for that just to keep their job from becoming boring and mundane. Keep the job as interesting as possible, as

Dr. Wayne Scott , J. Thomas Miller, III and Michele W. Scott

expansive as possible, and always let the worker know that you are behind him or her and supportive.

No one knows whether you motivate people on the job in this level but the cold facts are these – There are people who will rise to their level and will stay there.

In the book, *The Peter Principle*, the author tells us about the danger of promoting people above their level of competence. It is very difficult to motivate people once they have reached their level of competence and they are not ready to take the next step.

You can make the job more interesting, more expansive and let them learn a little at a time, but all people become stifled at one point. There are some people who just have to learn that they are not going to go any higher, and they adjust to this.

Abraham Maslow says there are five levels of needs – the physical, safety and securing, social, esteem, and self-actualized levels. The behaviorist Frederick Herzberg says that the physical level has to do with one's personal life, salary, benefits and so on, and the safety and security level has to do with company policy, supervision and technical skills.   On a social level are the needs for interpersonal relationships and advancement. The esteem level overlaps with interpersonal relationships. There are recognition needs, the ego needs, in the person, the act of offering him or her the job even though you know he or she would not take it.

In the actualizing need there is the work itself – the achievement and the growth potential inherent in any job. The place where we have the problems isn't down in the physical, safety and security needs. Even with our air, water and food needs, the fact remains that we don't have to work. It is not benefit programs -- no it is not really even social security. These aren't the problems. We have taken care of these. **The motivational areas in which we seem to be most inept are social, esteem and self-actualizing.**

How do we make a person feel viable, meaningful, a part of, accepted by, integrated with and recognized? How do we offer a person an achievement level in his or her life that is going to make them feel worthy, meaningful and viable? These are the areas of your inner self. The social area is less of a problem than esteem or self-actualizing. You probably socialize pretty well in you organization but you, as an individual, have your esteem and actualizing needs. **Esteem and self-actualizing are our motivational profit areas.**

Motivating On The Self-Actualizing Level

How do you get other people motivated on the esteem level or the self-actualizing level or the social level? It is apparent that you are going to have to know yourself first. Where are you on the "Maslow" ladder? You will need to know where every single person in your employ is on the ladder, or you are not going to really be able to make it – not as a motivator. If you are working with someone on an esteem level and the person's needs are on a physical level, have you motivated that person? No. Why? You are using the wrong tools. If you have someone who is a self-actualized individual, like the "rate buster" and you are trying to motivate him or her in safety and security needs, are you really going to motivate that person? No. The "rate buster" has already passed your motivational methods.

How are you going to know where the person is on his or her hierarchy of needs? Motivation only takes place on a needs-meeting level. How are you going to know where the individual worker is unless you know this other person? You are not. Where the person happens to be will be inculcated within his or her situation. So you have to know the situation too. If you are trying to motivate a person on a physical level and you know yourself that this person is not really able to do the job that has been given, what do you do? If you know the situation, where his or her life is, then you know more how to motivate with regards to the tools available. In this case, just listen to the person. By offering the job, saying, "You know, John, you would have gotten the job except we both know – you know and I know – that you wouldn't be comfortable in that job." This is a tool you have available. Honesty is a tool. You need to use it as a tool.

When we have met the basic physical needs, the challenge comes in meeting the needs of the ego, esteem and self-actualization so that the person becomes as big in his or her own eyes as they can in the job.

Superintendent Of Vertical Transportation

A man was working in a 20-story warehouse as the elevator operator – going up and down all the time. He had needs just like anyone else does: physical needs, safety and security needs, social needs, ego needs and self-actualizing needs. He has been with the company 15 years and is happy with what he does. He likes his job. He knows more about where things are stored in the 20-story warehouse than anyone else. Everyone is pleased with his performance. He is satisfied with his pay. His benefit program is good. He is on a first-name basis with everyone there.

All of a sudden one afternoon, while he relaxed at home, his little girl, who is now in junior high school, says, "Tell me Daddy, what do you do? What is your job?" He says he is an elevator operator. She replies, "Is that all you are? Is that all you do? Mary's daddy is a doctor. Sue's daddy is a banker. And you are just an elevator operator?"

You know how unreasonable adolescents can be. The man got to thinking about it and thought maybe his daughter was right. He began to wonder about his job. The next morning he thought, there is nothing good about my job. It is hurting my little girl and our relationship, so he went to his supervisor and turned in his resignation with a two-week notice. When questioned about the matter, he said he had a nothing job and his little girl was not satisfied with the kind of nothing job he had. When asked about pay and benefits, the fellow said everything was fine.

When the personnel manager thought about getting a replacement for this worker, he realized no one else would know as much about the job. Who was going to run an elevator all day long, up and down, and be as outgoing, friendly, nice and knowledgeable as this man? The boss went into a panic. The company didn't want to lose this man. The Vice President of Industrial Relations came down and they had a meeting. They found an old closet downstairs and cleaned it out, put a rug on the floor and outfitted it with a big desk, nice lamp, a couple of chairs and telephone. On the outside of the door they put a title. The next morning when the fellow came to work, they told him he had been promoted. He was now the Superintendent of Vertical Transportation. That met his ego needs; that met his esteem needs; that met his self-actualizing needs. He could go home and tell his daughter that he now had a title – he was more than just an elevator operator.

Now in some industries, such as textiles, everyone has new job titles. You are not a weaver anymore you are a textile constructioner. You are not a loom fixer anymore you are a textile mechanics specialist. Everyone has come up with a new job title that sounds very impressive. It meets needs, you see? It meets needs in people's lives on an ego level.

The truth is that motivation cannot be applied to everyone equally. It is a uniquely individual process. **More than any other single thing, motivation is a supervisor's job.** Supervisor success lies with your ability to be a motivator.

The Worker 15,000 Years Ago?

Let's look at the mistakes we made in the past, and consider man's view of himself stemming back some 15,000 years in the work process. At that time two people -- the preacher and the politician -- were released from the tribe in order to promulgate the rules, the regulations, the meanings, the purposes of the tribe, so that the tribe had enough air, water and food to survive. This was when man was running around with a stick looking for something to eat and that is all. Of course, 15,000 years ago man was not as civilized as he is now. He has become more civilized over the past few years than he has ever been before – 15,000 years ago all man wanted was air, water and food. He ate to work and he worked to eat. His work was looking for something to eat. And that is all he worked for. Everyone worked – man, woman and child. They thought about nothing but how they were going to satiate that gnawing ache in their bellies.

What happened was, as *Thomas Maltheous a sociologist has said, "There had been no such thing as human progress until man had a surplus of life-giving energy sustenance -- water, air, wheat, any kind of foodstuffs to keep his body going physically."*

Let's create an imaginative situation of about 15,000 years ago and bring it all from there. Two bands gather, one from the East and one from the West. All of a sudden, they come to this great big tract of almost-Eden. It is a beautiful place, fish a plenty, trees with fruits, all kinds of

125

wild herbs – all they can eat and a stream in the middle. It is as if they say, "Look, we have everything we need to survive right here."

There is Tribe A and Tribe B. There is only one leader in each tribe. The leader is the "Shaman" in each tribe. The "Shaman" helps the people to stay out of trouble with the gods, and begins to literally live off the fat of the land. He or she sees how things work in a growth process – something drops from a tree, it gets covered up, watered, something else grows, and so on. People learn to grow their own food through observation. Then comes animal husbandry, and they figure this out. Well, once they begin to get a surplus of food, they start to think of other things. They start things like organization and aesthetics. They start thinking about learning and promulgating the culture. They then really even start thinking about sex. Prior to this they were either too weak or too thirsty to think about sex. Sex is not primary until everything else is taken care of. The leaders begin to wonder about educating the tribe. How they will promulgate becomes a concern, and as we suspect, sooner or later these two tribes meet in the middle. (Recall each tribe has only one leader, the "Shaman.") What happens when they start meeting in the middle? Tribe A says, "This is mine," and Tribe B says, "No, it is mine." What happens then? They have a war. As a result of battle, one of the tribes wins. The other tribe becomes subservient to it.

Another thing happens – a new kind of leader emerges. In this battle, one guy was bigger, stronger, meaner, beat people to death quicker, and everything else. He became another kind of leader – he was the warlord. Now the band has two leaders, the warlord and a "Shaman" or priest. In today's world, these are the preacher and the politician. These were the first two people released from the tribe to think, to plan, to organize, to set down rules, to establish regulations, to think up ideas and to give directions in order to keep the life of the tribe going. What kind of rules, regulations, ideas and directions did they come up with? Whatever it took to organize these tribes to keep them working to maintain the surplus of air, water and food.

One of the rules was – If you don't work, you don't eat. Then there was the specialization process. Women did one thing; men did something else. Believe it or not, except in the last few hundred years women did almost everything while men did almost nothing. Over a long progression, this was what happened. In order to maintain rules, regulations and control they had to have a view of "man." Values? Before you can control man, you have to decide what he is. What kind of creature is he? They said, "He is a hungry creature. What he wants is to sustain his physical body. What he fears worse is death. Therefore, if he doesn't do what we tell him to do, we will kill him." So...capital punishment entered the picture rather early. Then they had to come up with sociological rules. They became more interested in how to control the group and direct them. They taught us our images of ourselves. *They are the ones who taught us to be dependent and taught us to not make waves – to maintain the status quo and not upset anything.*

Down through the ages the preacher and the politician, the first two released from the tribe to think, to organize, to promulgate the life of the tribe, had to come up with rules of control. And in order to control the tribes so that the tribes would continue to promulgate the foodstuffs, they had to have certain kinds of punishment. The tribal punishments were commensurate with their worth, values, meanings, purpose. They gave man their value system.

Today we are still viewing man in pretty much the same way as we did back then. Control is necessary to maintain air, water and food to survive. You don't work you don't eat. Unless you want to get naked in the street as was described in Chapter 3. Control of the tribe by the preacher and the politician took place in the value system. Value systems bestow worth on people – worth with regard to duty, actions, behavior. If they were trying to promulgate the life of the tribe, who was the most worthy person, the most valuable person in the tribe? Was it the person who harvested the most or the person who caused the most to be produced? Today, who is the most worthy, viable, looked-up-to, valuable person? The most productive worker is the one who is most highly prized.

Everything started back then by these two, the "Shaman" and the warlord, and they have totally dominated the life of mankind upon this earth ever since. *You may want to live under a 15,000-year-old system today but it is not possible to motivate people on the same basis.* **They motivated people by fear of losing the right to be in the tribe, the right to be a part of the tribe, the right to live. Today our motivational approach must exclude fear.**

Adam, Eve and Work

Where did the advent of work come from? Where did work start? How did it happen? There were two people on earth, Adam and Eve. What did they do? Eve *supposedly* stepped out of line and took Adam with her. We have been caught in this trouble ever since. What happened as the result? What was the punishment? You would sustain your life not from the fat of the land but from the sweat of your brow. Work then became a punishment, a curse as well as a necessity. Work became a necessity because it was a curse. There are some people who still see work that way? A curse. Is work really that? The truth is that seeing work as a curse means people do not like to do it. Therefore, we come up with two views, "Theory X" and "Theory Y" as will be discussed in the next chapter.

Summary Messages...
Motivation And How It Applies To You And Your Job

1. Achievement is wrapped up in three separate words – Creativity, Initiative and Enthusiasm.
2. Whatever the achievement is to you, it will never come unless you bring it about.
3. Performance equals Ability times Motivation.
4. The biggest single mistake we have made as managers with regard to motivation is the belief that you can take a motivation blanket, throw it out over your entire organization, let it settle down and motivate everyone the same way.
5. The four things you must know to motivate are: yourself; the other person; the situation of both the organization and the worker; and the tools available to you to meet the needs of the organization and the worker.
6. The only thing a supervisor can do realistically is to offer workers a stage upon which they can enact themselves to self-actualization.
7. The motivational areas in which we are presently having the most difficulty are: Social, Esteem and Self-Actualization.

6

Putting It All Together- The "12 Keys" For Motivating Today's Worker

The Genesis View Of Man

There is the "X theory" of work and the "Y theory" of work as described by Douglas McGregor. The X theory of work stems from the 15,000-year-old view – a pure Genesis view of man. What kind of view do you get of man from Genesis? When you talk about human relations, you understand you are also talking about motivation, because human relations and motivation go together. When you talk about human relations and motivation you have to talk about it three ways, not just one way – theologically, sociologically and psychologically.

The Theological View Of Man

Theology was first. Remember the priest and the politician – all rules and regulations, do's and don'ts, thou shalt's and thou shalt not's, right and wrong, immoral and moral. These were all handed down for us by these two people. They totally dominated the life of mankind upon this earth. They did it through assigning value to man. Value being what man does. If you have to have a view of man to motivate him commensurate to what he is, what you must have is an "X theory" of work that has been with us for years and years.

Can you remember in industry when, if people didn't perform as they should, they could be hung out the window. The very least they heard was, "Pick up your paycheck and get out of here," and then the boss sent for one of the people standing at the front gate waiting for a job! Can you remember when that was the way it was? Does that make it right? No. But it shows an inerrant view of the worth of people. They did not perform, so kick them out and don't ask why. Like the tribe -- you don't work you don't eat. Same thing. We are living in a time of change, but we still have a lot of people who see supervision that way. *From a pure "X" point of view people are economic first and foremost. They are economic; they are bad; they are lazy; they are unmotivated; they are selfish; they are lax; they are sinful;*

they hate work. In fact, they see work as a curse. If you have this view of man, what do you do? You come up with personnel policies, standard operating procedures, rules, regulations and time clocks that attempt to regulate.

Is that trust or is that seeing a worker as "theory X" type? You think if you don't have the time clock, he or she is going to take advantage of you. It is the same view of a worker that the supervisor had who said, "He won't work out. He just won't work out. He is a sinful, undone, unredeemed Genesis-viewed man living with that woman, and they are not even married. Therefore, if this is what he is doing, he is no good." It is a view of man handed down to us. It is a theological view. Now, there are a lot of people who see this as absolute. That is the way man is. He or she needs strong leadership, and has to have this strong leadership. We call this "stoking." "Stoking" will be for the theory X person and "stroking" will be for the theory Y person (see Figure 6-1).

The Social View Of Man

On the other hand, there is a "Y theory" of work. The "Y theory" says that a person is social. He or she is inherently good and wants to work even if independently wealthy. That person would still find something to do because of his or her hierarchy of needs, one of which is to feel actualized. One of the areas in which we can be actualized is viable performance and achievement with life on a day-to-day basis. You would work if you didn't have to, so the "Y theory" there is correct. The "Y theory" supervisor believes the worker wants to work, is

MOTIVATION

<u>Stoking</u> (X)	<u>Stroking</u> (Y)
· LAZY	· ACTION
· THREATEN	· SELF-MOTIVATED

· AVOID
  RESPONSIBILITY
	· SEEKS
	  RESPONSIBILITY

· ECONOMIC ANIMAL	· SOCIAL CREATURE

BASIC ANTHROPOLOGY

Figure 6-1. "Stoking" versus "Stroking"

industrious, and is self-motivated. They have good relationships -- societal relationships. He or she needs these relationships. Not only that, the worker is self-motivated, so when we have this as an absolute, we come up with standard operating procedures to do, to prove, to show -- not to control.

Remember in the beginning of this book the story told about a meeting where one person stood up and said, "I could care less if the worker lives or dies." And the other person got up and said, "You are crazy." This was at the beginning of Chapter One. That's when one side of supervision sees motivation in terms of the absolute "X" and the other side sees it as an absolute "Y" – that creates division. When we see supervision in terms of absolutes, we become divided.

If you don't believe there is a division go to a meeting where you have an age span of 25 to 55. You will see the division take place in a personnel meeting where you are talking about rules, regulations, procedures, policies, new kinds of things to enact for the worker, for the personnel, for the employee. Many people will be pure "Y" oriented. Others will be pure "X" oriented. In the meeting there will be a division of idealization. Some are thinking one way, others are thinking another way. Usually the older person has been taught "theory X" and the younger person "theory Y." But the truth is we are neither all "X" nor all "Y."

What we need is not an absolute "Y theory" of supervision, which is "stroking," or an absolute "X" view of supervision, which is "stoking." We need a new kind of supervisor, one who sees both a social and economic

Dr. Wayne Scott , J. Thomas Miller, III and Michele W. Scott

person. One who sees the total person. We are sometimes "X" – times when we are lazy, unmotivated and even selfish. We are sometimes "Y" – times when we are social and good. We are neither of these all the time, but a combination of these. What does that depend on?

Which is most important with regards to motivation – social or economic? The "X" supervisor represents the economic person and the "Y" supervisor represents the social person. Neither of these is correct, and yet both are correct! They are correct when we see a person in total – as a social and economic being. If we are to motivate a worker, we have to know which is most important in his or her life – the social aspect or the economic aspect. We have to know the worker and know the situation of the worker. Which of these is most important or which receives the most weight? It is kind of a seesaw. The person's situation at any given time in his or her life dictates whether one side or the other is weighted. When you leave home for work each morning, you leave with a certain set of life circumstances. You can receive one phone call during your workday and you can go from an economically motivated person to a socially motivated person – related to the predominance of the social or economic need in your life.

There is no such thing as a situation that is static. Do you have a situation, a life situation that has not changed in a year? Everyone's life is dynamic; everyone's life is changing. So the situation is dynamic. This being the case, then what is the most important thing to motivate anybody? *The most important thing to motivating anyone is to know that person's situation.* If you are going to motivate that

136

person on the basis of his or her situational needs at any given time, be aware that situational needs are changing and dynamic and are not static.

Consider this illustration. Here is Joe who makes minimum wage. His wife Edith cannot work because they have 18-month-old twins. They had four other children before the twins for a total of six kids and two dogs. They live in a six-room house. They are barely making it. Both the wife and the husband are only children. One day at work Joe gets a long-distance phone call. His mother has had a massive heart attack and she is in the hospital. He has to go there immediately. The outcome is that his mother is an invalid for the rest of her days. There is nowhere else for her to go. Joe's father is dead and the only thing that can happen is for his mother to move in with Joe's family. Joe and Edith move two kids out of a room, give the room to Mama, and double the kids up in other rooms. When Joe comes into work you notice the change in his attitude, but you are not really sure what the change is. He continues to work, but what does the guy need? "Stoking" or "stroking?" "Stroking?" No! He needs stoking. What is Joe's main concern right now? Where is he going to get the money to take care of this situation? What he really needs at the moment is some way to meet the financial obligations that he has had thrust upon him by the fickle finger of fate. You cannot know he needs that unless you know his situation. You cannot know what tools are available to you.

If that is not bad enough, Edith's mother falls, breaks both hips, and becomes an invalid. Guess where she moves? Right! Responsible Edith and Joe! Also, guess what? For

137

Dr. Wayne Scott , J. Thomas Miller, III and Michele W. Scott

forty years Joe and his mother-in-law have never gotten along. Now this guy is in more trouble than ever. Does he need "stroking" or "stoking?" You betcha he does need "stoking!"

You know Joe's situation. What tools are available to you to meet the needs of this person's life? What have you got? Overtime, right? Any odd jobs that you know of anywhere -- provided you know this man well enough. You can help him get a job where he can utilize his talents off the workplace. If you know him well enough you know what he can do. You can be on the lookout for extra work for him or for any way you can help. Extra work is a tool available to you. So are the tools of listening and caring. You will never "stroke" him in this situation unless you help his need – "stoking." He comes in three months later, walks up to you, the boss, with tears in his eyes, and says, "Well, Mama just passed away." So you know two things immediately. One, you know he is hurt; two, you know he is relieved. You give him his three days off and he takes care of the funeral. He comes back. He works, but he is still almost as distracted as before. Joe comes in two months later and says, "My mother-in-law died."

You know two things: he is hurt and he is relieved. You have been with him the whole time. You have let him talk to you; you have helped him; you have done everything you could. You sent him to banks; you helped him with credit unions; you have given him overtime. You have given him odd jobs. You've done everything you could.

One day two months later Joe walks in about two-feet high off the floor. He slaps you on the back and says, "Boy, let

138

me tell you something. My Mama had an insurance policy that I didn't know anything about. She left me $40,000. If that wasn't good enough, my wife's Mama had a policy that paid us $30,000." All of a sudden the guy has gone from nothing to $70,000! **Now he needs what? He needs "stroking."** His situation has changed, really changed. If you saw him through his time of need, he will see you through your time of need. A guy who has been working for minimum wage and then comes into a windfall is going to seek your advice and counsel about what to do with his windfall because you are his friend, particularly if you saw him through all his problems. He is going to hold on to the job that took care of him when he really needed taking care of. The key here is to know what the situation of a worker's life is so that you can know what the need of the person's life is. **If you do not know the situation, you cannot motivate.**

When is the last time someone rushed up to you and said, "I have got to tell you about my situation"? Probably yesterday. But how much of his or her real situation did that person tell you about? A person comes in and says, "Let me counsel with you," but do you really understand the situation? We must know the situation. There are no shortcuts. **In fact, there are twelve specific steps or twelve keys to motivation using successful human relations. These twelve keys incorporate all that has been presented to this point in this book.**

Dr. Wayne Scott , J. Thomas Miller, III and Michele W. Scott

The Psychological Approach ... Twelve Keys To Motivating Today's Worker

We are not going to talk about motivation in terms of Abraham Maslow, Frederick Herzberg or anyone but Wayne Scott and Thomas Miller. *This will not be theoretical but pragmatic advice.* **This will be a psychological approach specific to the degree that you can have an influence on workers' lives to get them to help you know them so that you know their situation.** You must know the situation of the company and of the worker so that you can know the tools available. These tools are summarized in Figure 6-2 and discussed below:

1. What is the **key to productivity? Only People.**

2. What is the **key to people producing? Positive Human Relations.**

3. What is the **key to positive human relations? Understanding.**

One weekend I took a book 870 pages long and I devoted myself to the task of reading it cover to cover. It was hot summertime. I thought while I am fishing and in the boat, I will read it. I almost lost the fishing rod in the process. I was so disappointed in the book that I threw it in the water. I read 870 pages in a book that told me only three things that I already knew. It told me three things – **the key to productivity is people** (some 200 pages), -- **the key to people producing is positive human relations** (some 300 pages) -- and **the key to positive human relations is**

140

understanding (another 300 pages). The problem to be solved – How does one get the understanding? *The book had assumed understanding. You cannot under any circumstances whatsoever assume understanding. Understanding has to happen. It happens in a methodical way that you can bring about.*

4. What is the **key to understanding**? **Knowledge.**

5. What is the **key to knowledge**? Does it just happen? No. **Revelation is the key.** You revealing to someone else or them to you.

6. What is the **key to revelation**? **Openness.**

7. What is the **key to openness**? **Sharing.**

Visualize if you will, a door that is almost closed. My hand is on the knob. You are a worker who comes to see me, your supervisor, after a weekend. You look through the crack in the door and you say, "I went fishing this weekend." You haven't shared much with me and I don't know a whole lot about you, but I do know you like fishing. If you continue by saying, "I went fishing and caught a five-pound big-mouth bass on a two-pound test line," what have you done? You have just opened the door a little more; you have begun to share with me; and you have opened that door just a little bit even though my hand is still on the knob – and slightly resisting being opened. I know you like fishing. I know you are proud of the fact that you caught a five-pound bass on a two-pound test line. It tells me that you are a skilled fisherman. It tells me that you get enthused about accomplishment, achievement and things like that. You think it was something to catch the bass on a two-pound test line.

Then you begin to tell me. "Guess what, my wife went with me, and we both killed two cases of beer while we were there." Well, you have opened the "door of sharing" a little further. At that juncture I can say, "Well, it's a darn shame you didn't drown, you drunkard!" Wham! The door closes. What have I done? I have closed the door. I have come down on you and found fault with your life, your style, and your values. I have censured or judged that which you were sharing with me, and you opened to the point that you gave me some insight into your life and your wife's. If I had kept my mouth shut, you might have opened it all the way, and said, "My daughter is pregnant, and I don't know who the daddy is!"

See? You might have opened all the way to **Revelation** and given me a chance to have a relationship with you. But the moment you said something I didn't like, I started to censure and make judgments. Bamm! I closed the "door of sharing" and I will never get to openness with you. As a supervisor I am never going to have enough knowledge to understand you as a person, so that I can exert true human relations on you in a need-meeting situation, to motivate you to be productive.

You see the continuity here and how one builds on the other. There are a lot of workers and supervisors who just cannot share. They don't know how to share; they are afraid to share. *If people don't share with you, it is because they don't have anything to share, or mostly because they are afraid if they do share, your life is so different from* *theirs that it would create censorship or judgment.* So the key to a person's sharing is very simple – **only a self-confident person will share.** A person will share with you only to the degree that he or she has enough self-confidence that if, in the sharing process, there is shown judgment, censorship and condemnation, he or she won't be so devastated that there is no personal identity left.

8. What is **the key to sharing? Self-confidence.**

Persons will share only to the degree of the self-confidence that they possess. They have to be confident enough in themselves that, if they share with you something about their lives, and you do censure them or judge them, it won't be so painful they cannot bear it. Self-confidence is where you really begin to build the whole process of motivation.

9. What is the **key to building self-confidence? Affirmation.**

I'll bet I can tell you who is the most significant other person in your life. I may not be able to call a name, but I can identify the person by the reason he or she is most significant. The most significant other person in your life is the person who affirms you the most – the person from whom you gain the most sense of being.

Affirmation, then, is the **key to self-confidence.** The person who affirms you most is the person who gives you a feeling of being confident. Confidence, then, is the end result of being affirmed. **You can see that you have the opportunity as a supervisor to be one of the most significant other persons in your workers' lives, especially if 80% of the workers are miserable**

143

everywhere except at work (recall family, politics and religion). Well, affirmation doesn't just happen. It is the result of something.

> 10. What is the **key to building affirmation** – what makes it possible? **Acceptance.**

One can affirm only that which one has first accepted. **Acceptance** then opens the door to the affirming process. Acceptance is not something we are taught. In fact we are taught to pass judgment on persons and their behavior. *By the time most of us are eight or ten all the acceptance that was inherently ours has been kicked out of us by family insistence, cultural dogma and religious values – "We will not drink or smoke or chew or go with girls who do."*

On the job this means the attitude we talked about earlier – "That guy can't work for me; he's living with a woman, and they aren't even married." **Unless you accept the person carte blanche you will never get the chance to change his or her behavior through affirmation – transforming that person into a productive member of the workforce.**

If acceptance is not a part of our normal behavior pattern, how then does it happen in you or me? First, we have to develop a new attitude about people and life in general. An attitude that says people are basically pretty good – are honest, are fair, have integrity – or at least have the potential for these qualities. You can call it a new humanism or open mindedness or tolerance or lack of being controlled by dogma. Mostly it is expressed very well in Thomas Harris's book titled *I'm O.K. – You're O.K.*

Therefore...

> 11. What is the **key to our acceptance** of ourselves and others? **The attitude that operates on an "I'm O.K. – You're O.K." level.**

Remember, a relationship can grow no deeper or grow no stronger than the sum total of the things each person in the relationship is willing to accept in the other. The one thing to remember is this – **If you cannot accept the worker as O.K., you will never have the chance to modify his or her behavior to a productive effort.**

Such an attitude in you and me does not happen easily. It does not come without effort and value changes. There is then a key to the "I'm O.K. – You're O.K." concept. Few people have it naturally. Most of us have to attain it on purpose.

> 12. What is the **key to gaining the "I'm O.K. – You're O.K." attitude? Training.**

(These steps are summarized in Figure 6-2.)

Remember we said: **A worker performs no better than his or her supervision allows, and his or her supervision is no more proficient than it is trained to be. Training, then, is the key.** It is training that becomes so important in your organization.

Recall the four things you must know to motivate anyone – **(1) you must know yourself; (2) you must know the**

Dr. Wayne Scott , J. Thomas Miller, III and Michele W. Scott

other; (3) you must know the situation; and (4) you must know the 12 keys (tools) available to you to meet the situation of both the company and the worker.

This being the case, you will motivate 90% of your workers 100% of the time and most specifically you will lead without intimidation and be respected at the same time.

To Motivate You Must Know
 1. SELF
 2. OTHER
 3. SITUATION
    a. other
    b. company
 4. Tools Available to Meet the Needs of 3 a, b.

12 STEPS (KEYS) TO MOTIVATION

 1. The KEY to Productivity – PEOPLE
 2. The KEY to People Producing – POSITIVE HUMAN RELATIONS
 3. The KEY to Positive Human Relations – UNDERSTANDING
 4. The KEY to Understanding – KNOWLEDGE
 5. The KEY to Knowledge – Revelation (Highest Degree of Self Disclosure)
 6. The KEY to Revelation – OPENNESS
 7. The KEY to Openness – SHARING
 8. The KEY to Sharing – SELF CONFIDENCE
 9. The KEY to Self Confidence – AFFIRMATION
10. The KEY to Affirmation – ACCEPTANCE
11. The KEY to Acceptance – I'M OK – YOU'RE OK ATTITUDE
12. The KEY to I'm OK You're OK – TRAINING

AFFECT
ON
PERSONS

SUPERVISOR

Figure 6-2. Twelve steps to Motivation

The Motivational Process

The motivational process is implemented in reverse of the above steps as follows i.e. #12 is implemented as #1, etc.

- You need to be constantly **trained** (#12) for your job.
- Through the training process you develop the right outlook on yourself, because you have to know yourself first and be able to say **"I'm O.K."**(#11) which lets you see the other as O.K.
- Then you can **accept**. (#10). No matter the attitude, no matter the person's background behavior or work. You can find something about them that is good, and can...
- **Affirm** (#9) whatever it is that is good about them.
- The more you affirm, the more **self-confidence** (#8) they will possess.
- The more self-confidence they possess, the more **sharing** (#7) that happens between you and them.
- The more sharing that happens, the more **openness** (#6) and **revelation** (#5) that occur.
- The more openness and revelation, the more **knowledge** (#4) you have.
- The more knowledge you have, the more able you are to **understand** (#3) this person's needs because you know his or her situation.
- The more you understand the better able you are to exert positive **human relations** (#2)...

- Only people (#1 step) are capable of increased productivity and performance through motivation . . . **MOTIVATION** enacted.

Don't let the simplicity of these steps obscure their significance. STUDY THEM, MEMORIZE THEM, then use them...one worker at a time...one step at a time!

I've seen supervisors set up file folders for each person working for them. Then they developed checklists and action plans for each step of the 12 steps. Over time and through personal and professional commitment of the supervisor...GREAT THINGS HAPPENED!

The supervisor became more significant to the worker and the worker become increasingly motivated.

A Case Study . . .A Problem To Solve

Consider this case history that took place in a small manufacturing company. This company manufactures caps and gowns from the process of purchasing the raw materials, taking orders by specific size, and then filling the orders according to the specifications. It is a very efficient manufacturing operation. It started out in a man's basement and grew to be a multi-million dollar business. There are several work sections. One is a folding and packaging table.

There is a woman at the folding and packaging table whose name is Lila. We know from her personnel records that she is 58 years old. Lila has been with the company for four years, and the company is only four and a half years old, so Lila has been there almost the whole time. Lila makes minimum wage. Lila works the table where the graduation gowns are laid at one end, folded, packaged, placed in a plastic bag, and finally placed in a box that goes to the shipping room in the back. The company has a problem at Lila's table and the problem is this: No one will work with Lila. Lila is abrasive, abusive and hostile. Her supervisors have done everything they can do with Lila. They have talked with Lila and have threatened to fire her. They have done everything. Lila thinks she's doing nothing wrong.

The station at the table looks like an assembly line where the merchandise is placed on a sliding mechanism that makes the caps and gowns pass along several workers. One person lays the gown on the table, one folds it, one places it into the plastic container, and another boxes it, and then the gown is moved to shipping. The work is reasonably simple. Not heavy work. Lila's responsibility along the assembly line is to stretch the gown to its fullest length, removing most wrinkles, prior to the next person folding the gown. The company cannot get any one to work on either side of Lila because as soon as they send someone back to her table, she starts in on the new worker. "Look, that is not the way you do it. Don't you know better than to fold it like that? That will be wrinkled when the kid opens it up for graduation. Don't do it like that. I have been doing this so long, I can do it in my sleep."

Lila does five times more than anyone else. She is never out, never late, never absent, she is always there. Anything you want done, you ask Lila. Lila will do it. She is one of the best workers you have got, but you cannot keep anyone working with her. They just will not do it longer than a day and a half at a time. Her supervisor has a real problem. Again, Lila can do by herself half again as much as all five of the other workers can do while they are there. She always exceeds production even if she has to stay over without even getting paid. They have done everything they know to help Lila get along with others. Now, what do they do? They've talked with her. They've said, "Lila, you have just got to get along with people." She doesn't get along with them any better. She exclaims, "It is not my problem. I do not say anything to those people. They just don't stay." How would you begin to approach a problem like this if you were her line supervisor?

A Solution

Let's go back and think for a moment of the twelve steps to motivation and the four things you have to know to motivate anyone to do anything. What do you have to know? Yourself, the other, the situation of the worker and the company, and the tools (12 steps) you have available to meet both. I asked her supervisor what he knew about Lila. He knew her age, how long she had been with the company and how much per hour she made. The supervisor did not know enough about Lila to do anything about this problem. He spent the next week finding out as much as he could about her. He knew Lila was abrasive, abusive and hostile, also he knew she was the best worker he had when it came to the work. However, he had decided if he could not train someone else to work on the table with Lila, he would have to get rid of her. That was his feeling. Now this company was family-owned and Lila was like part of the family.

However, Lila was creating a problem and everyone knew it.

The supervisor spent a whole week looking, asking, and talking. He found: (1) Lila is not married; (2) She has one child, who lives in New York City who rarely comes to see her and two grandchildren; (3) She lives in a trailer that is her own. She has been in this trailer four years. The only work Lila has ever done in her whole life, besides work in this company, is domestic work. Her only outside activity is church. She has no other real interests that her supervisor can discover. No real close ties outside the work area, no family, no husband, and she lives alone in her trailer. Now, knowing this, tells the supervisor something about Lila. She is lonely – and there are other things that he knows. She comes from a small southern town culture. He also knows that she has never had a job in her life that was anything but domestic. Probably the highest earning that she ever made was $50 a week. She kept the job until her mother died; then, she got this one when it became available.

What else? She is a loner and needs outside interests. She talked about **my** table, **my** job, **my** responsibility. Why does she think that way? What else does the supervisor know about Lila? She ran the table **by herself** before the company grew. She didn't just straighten the gowns -- she straightened, folded, wrapped, boxed and shipped. She did the whole thing, picked those cartons up and carried them out herself.

What would you say is the basic problem? Black or white, didn't seem to matter who worked with her. No one else had been there as long as she – no one. Her own taunt feelings of inadequacy are part of the problem, but it doesn't manifest itself in her being prejudiced. All of the other women were usually younger than Lila. Lila needs to feel needed and accepted.

The solution to the problem is in knowing Lila. The first thing you have got to do is know her. What motivates Lila to work? She runs her own household pretty much the way she runs her own job. However, she is insecure and threatened at work. She is scared that someone is going to take her job. She is threatened. When people become threatened, they act one of two ways – they either run or they fight. And when they fight, they become abrasive, abusive, hostile, and negative – and it is hard to live with them. Take away the threat, and Lila is no longer a problem.

I sat down with Lila and asked what the trouble was. "You are the best worker that they have, but no one can work with you." And she starts talking about how no one folds this right, or no one does this right, and so on. "It's not my fault that they can't do it!" Why? Because, if she can be indispensable, then she has job security. She is indispensable – it is just that no supervisor has handled her in such a way that they have taken enough time with her to let her see that she is indispensable. Lila felt so keenly about her job that tears came in her eyes when I asked her the question, "Lila, what does your job mean to you?" The first words out of her mouth were, "It means dignity. For the first time in my life, it means dignity. I am not someone's servant. I got dignity." Now a person will fight you to their death to maintain something like that –

153

something they found after 58 years. Lila now has an income that will allow her to be someone commensurate with her image of herself.

Not only that, but tears came to her eyes when she was explaining to me what her job meant to her in terms of the service it performed. She said, "You know, I never was educated myself. Never did go to school at all, but I know how these kids look forward to graduating from high school. They work hard for twelve years, they study and they learn. It wasn't easy, and this is the crowning day of their twelve years of school. I just think that when they put on this robe that I package, it ought to look really good." She said, "It is almost like I am having a part of what they are doing."

Now, uneducated or not, schooling or not, Lila had a lot of wisdom, and she was able to talk about the depth of something out of 58 years of experience that only comes when one has something very negative to contrast with it. She wanted her job because her job was her baby. It was her child. It was her life. She was one of those 90% whose job means more to them than any other single thing – contrasted with family, church and politics. The solution of the problem is to take away the threat. Lila doesn't have to continue to prove herself. She is not in competition with anyone. Her job is secure. In this case, Lila had to be shown that no one could take her job. She had a job that was secure, and she needed the job as much as the job needed her. It is beyond my comprehension that in four years no one had ever told her that.

After talking to Lila, I talked to the line supervisor and told him he had to make Lila feel that none of the other workers can take her job away from her. **The only thing he had to do was to make Lila feel needed.** He went to Lila and told her the company needed her, and the kids out there who were going to graduate needed her. "We are behind in production here, and no one can help us make it but you. Unless things get better here, we are not going to make some of the orders, and students are going to have to graduate without gowns." Lila asked what she could do. "Teach others to be as good as you, Lila. That is what you can do." So the suggestion was taken. They made Lila the lead person at the table and gave her fifteen-cents-an-hour raise. They let her see she was needed. And when the company was caught up with production, the supervisor wanted to do away with two of the people at her table. But, guess what? Lila said, "Them is **my** girls." It didn't take long for her to train them either. They got so efficient that Lila would bring in a cake for **her** girls. She would bring in lunch. Lila got to be the grandmother of all of them – and everything went along beautifully.

Lila is still there packing the graduation gowns. Her section finishes two hours before any other section does. The people are not being misused. Although they have two more people than they need, the supervisor is not going to take on Lila to get rid of them! The company has a good thing going – Why mess it up? All the supervisor had to do was make Lila feel needed and secure once they recognized the fact that she was lonely and threatened -- once they recognized the fact that her job gave her a sense of meaning, purpose, dignity, and, mainly, an independence that she had never had before. Such is important to a

155

Dr. Wayne Scott , J. Thomas Miller, III and Michele W. Scott

person where a job is concerned. It takes a certain kind of leadership to be able to see that. It takes a kind of leadership that can have feeling and caring for people.

Summary Messages...
Putting It All Together – The "12 Keys" To Motivating Today's Worker

The Supervisor (you) Affected. . .

1. You need to be constantly **trained** (#12 step) for your job.
2. Through the training process you develop the right outlook on yourself, because you have to know yourself first and be able to say **"I'm O.K."**(#11) which lets you see the other as O.K.
3. Then you can **accept**. (#10). No matter the attitude, no matter the person's background behavior or work. You can find something about them that is good, and can...

The Worker Affected . . .

4. **Affirm** (#9) whatever it is that is good about them.
5. The more you affirm, the more **self-confidence** (#8) they will possess.
6. The more self-confidence they possess, the more **sharing** (#7) that happens between you and them.
7. The more sharing that happens, the more **openness** (#6)
8. With more openness, then more **revelation** (#5) occurs.

The Supervisor Affected . . .

9. The more openness and revelation, the more **knowledge** (#4) you have.
10. The more knowledge you have, the more able you are to **understand** (#3) this person's needs because you know his or her situation.
11. The more you understand the better able you are to exert positive **human relations** (#2)...
12. Only **people** (#1 step) are capable of increased productivity and performance through motivation ⸪ . **MOTIVATION** *enacted.*

About The Authors

Dr. Wayne Scott is an acclaimed consultant, author, and internationally known platform speaker. He received his Ph.D. from The Ohio State University and is also a graduate of Harvard's Institute for Educational Management, and The University of North Carolina's School of Business Executive Development Program.

During the past 30 years, Dr. Scott has served as Senior Lecturer for the American Management Associations. He has served both as a corporate and college president. Also, he has authored numerous articles, publications, books on human motivation, self-directed behavioral change and leadership including his latest book " *Creating Success: Leadership in an Academic Organization* ".

Presently Dr. Scott serves as Chief Operating Officer of the Covington-Newton Campus of DeKalb Technical College.

J. Thomas Miller, III served as Dean of the Management Division of Greenville Technical College from 1973-1978. He is a past Senior Lecturer for the American Management Associations and past lecturer for the University of Southern California Management Safety School. His course "Effective Management/Leadership Techniques" has been received with enthusiasm in all areas of the United States, The United Kingdom, Germany, Switzerland, South Africa, Kuwait and Canada.

Presently, Tom Miller is President of Leadership Seminars Associates a company he founded in 1974.

His latest book is entitled, *"Making It In Spite of . . ."*

Michele W. Scott is a free-lance writer, behavioral modification and grief consultant. She is a graduate of the University of North Carolina at Charlotte with a Baccalaureate Degree in Social Work.

Printed in the United States
25011LVS00003B/296

9 780759 626591